KU-497-926

CONTENTS

Chapter One: An Overview

Chapter Two: The GMF Debate

Introduction

The GM Food Debate is the forty-seventh volume in the Issues series. The aim of this series is to offer up-to-date information about important issues in our world.

The GM Food Debate examines the controversial issue of genetically modified food.

The information comes from a wide variety of sources and includes:
Government reports and statistics
Newspaper reports and features
Magazine articles and surveys
Literature from lobby groups
and charitable organisations.

It is hoped that, as you read about the many aspects of the issues explored in this book, you will critically evaluate the information presented. It is important that you decide whether you are being presented with facts or opinions. Does the writer give a biased or an unbiased report? If an opinion is being expressed, do you agree with the writer?

The GM Food Debate offers a useful starting-point for those who need convenient access to information about the many issues involved. However, it is only a starting-point. At the back of the book is a list of organisations which you may want to contact for further information.

*****

The GM Food Debate

ISSUES

Volume 47

Editor

Craig Donnellan

Independence

Educational Publishers

Cambridge

First published by Independence
PO Box 295
Cambridge CB1 3XP
England

British Library Cataloguing in Publication Data
The GM Food Debate– (Issues Series)
I. Donnellan, Craig II. Series
363.1'92

ISBN 1 86168 194 1

Printed in Great Britain
The Burlington Press
Cambridge

Typeset by
Claire Boyd

Cover
The illustration on the front cover is by
Pumpkin House.

Genetically modified foods

Information from the Young People's Trust for the Environment

There has been much concern recently about GM foods, some of which are being tested and some of which are already used as ingredients in the food we eat. GM stands for 'genetically modified', and describes the process by which scientists are able to pinpoint the individual gene which produces a desired outcome, extract it, copy it and insert it into another organism.

To some extent, humans have been involved in genetic modification for centuries. For example, larger cattle which gave more milk were bred to produce even larger offspring. Seeds from cereals and other crops that were hardier and grew better were selected for planting the following year to produce better yields. With genetically modified organisms, however, the modifications involved are often of a kind that could not possibly occur naturally. For example, adding cow growth hormone to the embryo of a broiler chicken to produce a larger, faster growing chicken, or adding genes from a virus to a plant to allow it to become resistant to the virus.

There are many reasons why GM foods could be advantageous. For example, a crop could be made to grow quicker, with increased protein and vitamin levels, or with less fat. An often-used argument in favour of GM crops is that drought-resistant crops could help to alleviate famine in developing countries, where low rainfall often leads to food shortages. Techniques have also been developed to make fresh produce last longer, so that it can ripen on the plant and be transported more easily with less wastage.

The first GM food products – a tomato purée and a vegetarian cheese – appeared in British supermarkets in 1996. The purée was made from tomatoes which were designed to stay firmer for longer, leading to less waste in harvesting. The tomatoes also held less water, meaning that less water was required to grow them and less energy was used removing water from them to turn them into purée. This in turn made the purée cheaper for the consumer.

The first GM soya was planted in the US in the same year, and up to 60% of all products on supermarket shelves could now contain some GM soya. Monsanto, a major GM manufacturer, has developed a strain of GM soya which is resistant to Roundup™, its own brand of herbicide. This allows weeds to be controlled even after the soya has started to grow, saving an estimated 33% on the amount of herbicide used. Roundup Ready™ soya amounted to 15% of the 1997 US soya crop.

GM foods have been largely accepted by the Americans, with nearly 70% of them saying that they would buy GM foods even if they were simply engineered to stay fresh for longer. Even more would purchase foods modified to resist insect pests, resulting in less use of pesticides.

In the UK, we are being far more cautious, possibly with good reason. Lessons learned during the BSE crisis are still very much in people's minds. Can we trust what we are eating, and what could be the long-term effects?

We have potentially more to lose by the introduction of GM crops. In America, farming takes place on an industrial scale, with millions of acres used exclusively for growing crops. Intensive use of pesticides has virtually wiped out wild animals and plants in the huge crop fields of the US. The Americans can afford to do

Like a car manufacturer design to only run on it own brand petrol.

this, as they also have many huge wilderness conservation areas often the size of several English counties, which are havens for all their native wildlife. Here, however, farms are an integral part of the countryside. The use of herbicide- or insect-resistant crops could potentially have severe effects on our biodiversity, by virtually wiping out wild flowers and consequently the insects that feed on them, and further up the food chain, the predators that eat the insects.

Some crops are being developed to improve soil quality, by removing heavy metals from the soil, for example, so that they can be harvested and destroyed. An excellent idea, but what about the animals that eat the contaminated plants? Others are being developed for salt resistance, so that they can be grown in previously unusable areas. But what if their seeds were to be carried to a saltmarsh? Would they be a threat to wild species that have lived there naturally for years?

So far, there is no evidence of GM food being harmful to humans, but the rules governing their testing are less strict than with medicines, and after BSE, we know that 'no scientific evidence of harm' is not the same as 'safe to eat'. A report published last year by Dr Arpad Pusztai sparked off public fears about GM foods. He claimed that his experiments, which involved feeding rats with potatoes genetically modified with a lectin gene from a snowdrop, caused stunted growth and immune system problems for the rats.

Though his report has been heavily criticised by other scientists, the Royal Society, Britain's oldest and most prestigious scientific body, has recommended that more research is needed. Each new genetic modification needs to be extensively tested for its safety, for not only humans but also animals and plants. No single test taken in isolation can either legitimate or condemn all GM food, or indeed any single genetically modified organism.

Laboratory tests have shown that pollen from GM maize in the US damaged the caterpillars of the Monarch butterfly. This is a case of damage to a single species, but it

does show that genetically modified organisms could have the potential to do unexpected harm to other plants and animals. In the end, this could lead to a loss of biodiversity and to certain animal and wild plant species effectively being rendered extinct.

Where test crops have been planted in this country, there is a definite danger of cross-contamination with wild or non-GM plant strains. Even with very strict controls in place, it is impossible to prevent pollen from travelling on the wind from GM crops to other, possibly organic versions of the same crop being grown nearby. Pollen could also be carried by insects. This could mean that in the end, all our food crops could contain a proportion of genetically modified elements, and we as consumers would lose our right to choose whether to eat GM foods or not.

The countries most affected by drought and famine, which are purported to be potentially the greatest beneficiaries of GM foods, are not showing great enthusiasm for the newly developed crops. In fact, 20 African countries including Ethiopia have published a statement in which they claim that gene technologies will not help their farmers, but would 'destroy the

---

In the UK, we are being far more cautious, possibly with good reason. Lessons learned during the BSE crisis are still very much in people's minds

---

diversity, the local knowledge and the sustainable agricultural systems . . . and undermine our capacity to feed ourselves'. Some new strains of crop being developed by biotech companies have a 'terminator' gene built in to them to prevent farmers from keeping seeds produced by their crops for the following year. This could lead to complete dependence on the biotech company year on year, a very worrying development for farmers in poorer countries.

Whatever the potential gains for humanity, GM crops are being developed for profit. There may well be huge benefits to be had, but huge sums of money – currently billions of dollars – would not be invested in gene research if there were not the possibility of huge financial gains for the producers of GM crop strains in the future.

We quite simply do not know enough about the consequences for human, animal and plant life throughout the world of planting GM crops at the moment. More testing needs to be carried out, preferably by independent research bodies rather than biotech companies, before genetically modified organisms should be released into the world.

GM foods are not necessarily bad, but permitting the expansion of GM crop planting and use in our food without proper knowledge as to the effects, both short and long term, is at best unwise and at worst highly dangerous. It's not just we humans who could suffer, but ultimately many animal and plant species as well. Can biotech companies really be sure that their products will have no undue effects on biodiversity and food chains, and indeed on people's health? Until they are, the mass introduction of GM crops should not be permitted. We must proceed down the route of genetic modification with extreme caution, without denying that in some cases there could be great benefits to be had.

• The above information is an extract from the Young People's Trust for the Environment's web site which can be found at www.yptenc.org.uk

Pros and cons

Genetically modified food. Information from the Society, Religion and Technology Project

Some see genetic engineering opening up great opportunities in agriculture, food and medicine, as we learn to harness the power of the gene. For others it's a threat to something very basic about ourselves and the natural world, unnecessary, harmful, unethical, and mostly benefiting big business at others' expense.

In the midst of the controversy what are the real issues?

The objections

Should we be modifying genes at all?
- It's 'playing God' or unnatural.
- It's wrong to mix genes from radically different organisms.
- Religious and vegetarian groups would object to genes from some species.
- Do we really know what we're doing?
- Have we evaluated the risks sufficiently?

Is it really necessary?
- Do we need genetically modified food?
- It is just going to provide luxuries for the rich, and won't feed the Third World.
- Agriculture is already too tech-

Society Religion and Technology Project

nological. This will only make it worse.
- There are better ways to improve resistance and reduce chemicals on the land.

Do we have a real say in what's going on?
- Labelling measures are inadequate, and unjust towards those who object.
- Big business is imposing on our freedom under the guise of free trade.
- Government committees do not represent ordinary people enough.
- Supermarkets act as enough of a voice.

The case in favour

We shouldn't be afraid of biotechnology
- Why draw the line here, not elsewhere?

- We have many safeguards in place.
- Changing one or two genes does not make a foodstuff unacceptable.
- We are more than just our genes.

Look at the opportunities for good
- Better resistance to weeds, pests, disease.
- Better texture, flavour, nutritional value.
- Longer shelf life, easier shipment.
- Better yield, more efficient use of land.
- Less herbicides and other chemicals.
- Essential if we are to feed the world.

The economic and employment case
- Opportunities for Scottish innovation to benefit the people of Scotland.
- If we pull out, jobs and wealth we might have created will go abroad instead.

The democratic case
- With labelling, adequate protection can be given for those who object.

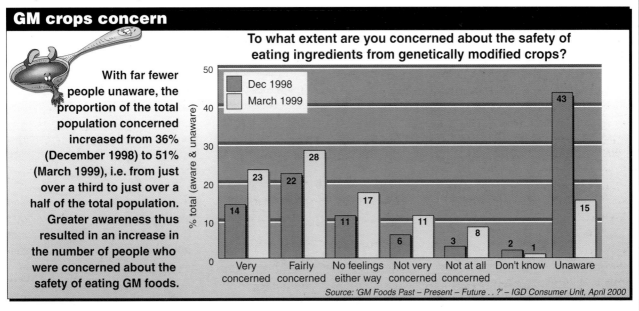

GM crops concern

With far fewer people unaware, the proportion of the total population concerned increased from 36% (December 1998) to 51% (March 1999), i.e. from just over a third to just over a half of the total population. Greater awareness thus resulted in an increase in the number of people who were concerned about the safety of eating GM foods.

To what extent are you concerned about the safety of eating ingredients from genetically modified crops?

- Dec 1998
- March 1999

% total (aware & unaware)

	Very concerned	Fairly concerned	No feelings either way	Not very concerned	Not at all concerned	Don't know	Unaware
Dec 1998	14	22	11	11	3	2	43
March 1999	23	28	17	6	8	1	15

Source: 'GM Foods Past – Present – Future . . ?' – IGD Consumer Unit, April 2000

- Several ethics and safety advisory committees represent public concerns.

Should we be doing genetic modification?

Some Christians object in principle to genetically modified food, as an unacceptable intervention in God's creation violating barriers in the natural world. Others see the potential for using God's gift of our technical skills, but with strong provisos, on matters of food safety and environmental risk. Christians believe that all of God's creatures are much more than their genes. To change one or two genes wouldn't make an organism less than itself, unless the change itself caused a major disruption. Ethical problems may arise for certain types of gene, for example animal genes for a vegetarian or pig genes for a Jew or Muslim. Such products are not envisaged, out of respect for these questions. Before a gene is transferred from one organism to another it is copied millions of times, so the chances of eating the same gene are tiny, but a pig gene doesn't cease to be pig by copying it. What matters to most is where it originally came from, and the genetic information, which is still the same.

Problems with genetically engineered soya bean and maize imports

The first main genetically modified food was a tomato paste, introduced with careful consumer consultation, clearly labelled. It sold well until the current furore began. In 1996 the EU accepted the import of US genetically modified soya bean and maize, staple commodities which go untraced into a large number of processed foods. The US companies refused to label or segregate the new products, more concerned with winning markets than public attitudes. Ordinary people ended eating modified food without knowing it, with no tangible benefit to them, and having no real say in the decisions. This major failure of democracy resulted in a huge consumer backlash. It also raised questions of environmental risks of GM crops spreading genes to other

species and possible loss of bio-diversity. These risk issues will be addressed in a new SRT information sheet.

Who benefits, who loses? – labelling and segregation

Food is a special case. Anyone wanting to make substantial changes to what we are offered to eat must take the greatest care to listen to the public and respect their views. Those with objections to genetically modified food must be given the option of not eating it, and should not have to pay more for what till now has been 'normal' food. EU legislation is unjust in requiring labelling only if foods contained identifiable levels of foreign DNA or proteins. This is irrelevant to the many people who object on ethical or environmental grounds to the fact that genetic modification had been used in the process. They have no choice but to eat what they object to. This injustice needs to be righted by a change in the law, with mandatory labelling by process, and proper segregation of source materials.

Will genetic engineering really feed the world?

Claims are often made for the potential of genetically modified food to 'feed the world'. If genes could be manipulated to enable staple crops to grow in what are today marginal conditions, it might make a big difference to many countries which struggle to feed themselves. However,

Christians are concerned that the driving forces of biotechnology are leading us to create unnecessary products for western indulgence, when the real food shortages else-where in the world remain neglected. Technically these areas are proving difficult, and financially there is less return than products for our super-markets. If the claim to feed the world is not to be mere propaganda, biotechnological investment and expertise needs a radical re-orientation to the specific needs of marginal agriculture in the Third World. At present it is just another 'rich man's' technology. Often the best solutions will be better breeding with their own indigenous resources, rather than high-tech solutions which may be inappropriate. What-ever is done must be in sensitive collaboration with local com-munities. Exploitation by multi-national agrichemical and seed corporations, more interested in market share than people, is another reason for bringing these tech-nologies into a proper public accountability.

- For more information about this and other ethical issues in tech-nology, contact: Society, Religion and Technology Project , Church of Scotland, John Knox House, 45 High Street, Edinburgh EH1 1SR. Tel 0131 556 2953, Fax 0131 556 7478. E-mail : srtp@srtp.org.uk or visit their web site at www.srtp.org.uk

The concerns

Information from the Food Commission

THE
FOOD
COMMISSION
Publisher of the Food Magazine

Is it safe?

Opponents of genetic modification argue that we do not know enough about the science and that altering genes could lead to unforeseen problems for future generations.

Supporters of the technology argue that strict controls are already in place and each modified product is very thoroughly assessed for any difference from its conventional counterpart. In addition, since it only utilises the genes for a specific trait, the technology is far more precise than the trial-and-error approach of traditional plant and animal breeding.

What laws exist?

In the UK, the Food Safety Act requires that all food must be fit for consumption, i.e., must not be injurious to health, be unfit or contaminated.

A specific set of safeguards controls the use of genetic modification in foods or food ingredients. The Novel Foods and Novel Food Ingredients Regulations 1997 implement the EU Council Regulation on novel foods. This requires that before novel foods and ingredients are placed on the market they must be assessed for safety.

In the UK these foods are assessed by a number of Committees. The Committees, which were active well before implementation of the EU Regulation, are made up of independent experts, including consumer representatives. They are mainly responsible for advising Ministers about individual applications with regards to the safety of crops and food ingredients.

The Food Standards Agency is the principal recipient for this advice as part of its strategic responsibilities for advising on GM foods.

What about the environment?

A main concern is that genes incorporated into a plant could 'escape' and transfer to other species with unwanted consequences. For example, it is argued that herbicide tolerant crops could cross-pollinate with weeds to produce herbicide tolerant 'superweeds'; or that the destruction of all weeds in the farm environment will reduce food sources for wild birds and animals.

Some consumers and farmers are concerned that making crops herbicide tolerant might lead to an increase in herbicide use, as future generations of crops may withstand higher doses of the herbicide.

Supporters of biotechnology argue that stringent rules exist to safeguard against these possibilities and that the development of genetically modified plants will mean a decrease in the use of environmentally unfriendly herbicides.

What laws exist?

UK regulations are:
- The Genetically Modified Organisms (Contained Use) Regulations 1992
- The Genetically Modified Organisms (Deliberate Release) Regulations 1992

These implement European Directives to control laboratory experiments, field trials and commercial use.

The UK regulatory bodies are the Health and Safety Executive and the Department for Transport, Local Government and Regions. The latter is advised by the Advisory Committee for Releases to the Environment (ACRE) which is responsible for assessing all applications for releasing genetically modified organisms into the environment in the UK. Part of the risk assessment involves field trials; these are strictly controlled but nevertheless remain controversial.

More strategic advice is provided to Government by the Agricultural and Environment Biotechnology

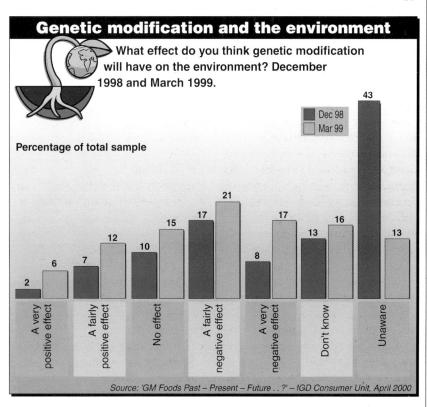

Genetic modification and the environment

What effect do you think genetic modification will have on the environment? December 1998 and March 1999.

Percentage of total sample

	Dec 98	Mar 99
A very positive effect	2	6
A fairly positive effect	7	12
No effect	10	15
A fairly negative effect	17	21
A very negative effect	8	17
Don't know	13	16
Unaware	43	13

Source: 'GM Foods Past – Present – Future . . ?' – IGD Consumer Unit, April 2000

Commission (AEBC). Its focus on biotechnology issues affecting agriculture and the environment includes the assessment of farm-scale evaluations, gene flow and biotechnological developments on animals.

Field trials are being carried out to evaluate the longer-term impact of GM crops on the UK environment. The biotechnology industry and growers have made a voluntary agreement with the Government that no GM crops will be grown commercially in the UK until those trials are completed.

Additionally the Government has made a commitment that the working of its Advisory Committees should be more transparent and that consumer interests must be taken fully into account, both through representation on the Committees and via public consultations. The extent to which consumers perceive that this is happening will be an important factor in determining whether or not they ultimately accept the technology.

What about labelling ?
Labelling is an important way of informing consumers about which foods and ingredients have been genetically modified. Consumers clearly want this information and *slowly* food manufacturers and retailers are responding. However, many complex issues are involved and it is taking considerable time to develop meaningful and enforceable legal rules. It is essential that these rules are agreed at EU level, which adds both an extra dimension and delay. Nevertheless some progress has been made and initial rules are in place.

The EU Regulation which governs the labelling of GM soya and GM maize establishes the principle that foods which contain any modified protein or modified DNA from the GM soya or maize crops must be labelled. These provisions are likely to be applied to any other GM ingredients approved by the EU in the future.

The Regulation also provides for a 'negative list' to be drawn up. This is intended to specify those products derived from GM soya or GM maize where it is known that neither modified protein nor modified DNA is present. For example, refined soya oil, refined maize oil and glucose (derived from maize starch). Such products will be exempt from GM labelling.

The requirement to label when any modified protein or modified DNA is present is very strict. This is a departure from previous rules which would only have required labelling if the foods concerned were 'no longer equivalent' to their conventional counterparts if, for example, they had a different use or nutritional value. Such tightening up of the rules reflected widespread consumer demand.

Even so, the Regulation still left gaps. For example, food additives and flavourings fell outside the scope of the labelling requirement and this was criticised. This prompted further regulations, which cover additives and flavourings, and address the complex subject of identity-preserved ingredients.

• The above information is from *Food for Our Future – Genetic Modification and Food*, an information pack produced by the Food Commission. See page 41 for their address details.

© The Food Commission

The benefits

Information from the Food Commission

Plants
Currently 25% of the world's food crops are lost through insect attack every year; that's enough food to feed one billion people. Supporters of GM technology say that the development of GM crops could reduce these and other losses to our food supplies. GM technology could also improve the quality of the food produced. For example:

Disease and pest resistance
Genetic modification has already been used to make food crops resistant to diseases and pests. For example a variety of maize (corn), first grown in North America, is resistant to the corn borer insect

— THE —
FOOD
COMMISSION
Publisher of the Food Magazine

which can destroy up to 20% of a crop. The genetic make-up of the plant has been altered so that it produces a new protein which enables it to resist the insect. Approximately 25% of the 2000 US maize harvest was genetically modified in this way.

GM research is being carried out to make sweet potato plants resistant to the feathery mottle virus which often ruins two-thirds of the African sweet potato harvest. Cucumber, lettuce, tomatoes, peppers and other horticultural crops could be modified to resist the destructive cucumber mosaic virus.

Weed control
Weeds are a serious threat to our food crops and whilst many herbicides (weedkillers) are available they have certain limitations in practice. For example, when growing soya, general purpose (broad spectrum) herbicides – which kill a range of weeds – can only be used before the crop emerges from the soil. Once the crop is visible, selective (narrow spectrum) herbicides have to be used to combat weeds without

damaging the growing soya crop.

Several varieties of soya have been genetically modified to tolerate the general purpose herbicide glyphosate. Farmers can therefore control weeds amongst the growing soya plants and choose the optimal time at which to spray.

It is claimed that less glyphosate is needed to control the weeds compared with selective weedkillers. Using fewer chemicals is considered better for the environment. There are potential energy savings too; the use of tractor diesel is reduced as fewer sprayings mean fewer trips across the fields. It is further claimed that the GM soya crop produces higher yields.

Approximately 50% of the 2000 US soya harvest was GM soya.

Feeding the world
The global requirement for food is set to double in the next two generations and the pressure on land use is rapidly increasing. Supporters of GM technology point out that it could help by increasing the quantity and quality of food produced, at less cost to the environment.

Critics of the technology question these claims and suggest that feeding the world depends on political solutions.

Improved nutritional value
Higher protein foods
Lack of protein is a major cause of malnutrition in many countries. Genetic modification could be used to enhance the protein content of crops such as rice.

Foods higher in vitamins and minerals
Some fruits and vegetables could be modified to contain higher levels of nutrients, for example, vitamins C and E. Rice, modified to increase supplies of iron and vitamin A, is in the pipeline for developing countries.

Longer-lasting fruit and veg
Genetic modification can slow down softening to produce fruits that last longer. Flavr Savr® tomatoes with this trait were the first GM food to be sold in the US. A similar tomato grown in California and made into tomato purée was one of the first

GM foods to reach the UK. Slow softening apples, raspberries and melon have also been produced and this trait is likely to be transferable to other fruits and vegetables.

Further examples
Other potential modifications could include:
- Maize, soya beans, oilseed rape (canola) and other oil crops modified to alter their fat content and composition.
- Peanuts modified so that they no longer cause the life-threatening reaction in those people who are allergic to the protein in them.
- Wheat modified to be gluten free – a benefit for those with coeliac disease.
- Bananas or other fruits modified to contain vaccines against cholera and hepatitis B.

Possible future developments
Drought resistance
Drought resistance in plants would enable farmers to extend both the growing season and number of places where crops could grow. This is not just a problem in hotter countries. Water availability is a limiting factor nearly everywhere plants are grown, even in the UK.

Nitrogen fixing
Plants need nitrogen to grow. Certain bacteria found in the roots of peas and beans can take nitrogen from the air and convert, or 'fix', it for use in plant growth. Scientists are trying to use GM technology so that these bacteria can live in the roots of cereal crops to provide a ready-made source of fertiliser. This could be cheaper and more environmentally friendly than the fertilisers we use today.

Frost damage
Frost damage can ruin many crops. Work is under way to produce plants with an inbuilt mechanism to help prevent frost damage. One possibility would involve utilising the genes in fish which enable them to tolerate extreme cold. However, the prospect of copying and transferring 'animal' genes to plants is very controversial. It remains to be seen if this would be acceptable to the public.

• The above information is from *Food for Our Future – Genetic Modification and Food*, an information pack produced by the Food Commission. See page 41 for their address details.

The debate nobody wants

Genetically modified food

By Paul Brown
Environment Correspondent

One of the biggest failures of Tony Blair's first term was missing the public mood on genetically modified food and crops.

Quite simply, following BSE, the public did not want their food mucked about with, and when they thought about it, their countryside either.

Despite this unprecedented revolt by consumers, Tony Blair, while avoiding mention of the issue at all, remains a GM enthusiast.

The fact that during his first term every supermarket chain has withdrawn genetically modified foods from its shelves and gone to extensive lengths to insist suppliers are GM free seems to have passed the prime minister by.

Currently there is no market in Britain for GM food and most chains are also banning GM crops from animal feed. Even Coca Cola is saying it does not want sugar from GM sugar beet in its drinks.

Despite all this, full-scale trials of genetically modified crops are under way, even though there is serious public opposition.

Even the food standards agency, one body set up to restore confidence in British food, seems happy to endorse GM products on the basis that they cannot find any danger to the public.

The only question still left in the government's mind is whether GM crops might damage the environment, and that answer will not be known until 2003, even if the current trials do manage to produce a result.

None of this grapples with the central problem that there is no gain in the technology for the consumer and only perceived threats.

If politicians believe that GM food and crops are the future they should be prepared to discuss the issues with environment groups and allay public fears

Why they should be talking about it

GM as an issue is not going away. Britain has a lot of expertise and money invested in the biotech industry, and potentially a lot of jobs. The future of British farming, whether organic agriculture has a future, and the shape of the countryside are all tied up in the the debate.

The perception that the prime minister is a pushover for big business interests is partly tied up with his perceived lack of interest in genuine public concerns about the consequences of embracing this technology. So far multi-national companies controlling GM patents appear to be the only winners from the GM revolution, at least as far as the farmer and consumer are concerned. If politicians believe that GM food and crops are the future they should be prepared to discuss the issues with environment groups and allay public fears.

What could be done?

The government claims the technology is safe but there is no liability regime in place if anything goes wrong. GM companies should be required to provide insurance to indemnify farmers against successful claims from organic producers and beekeepers if they lose their markets because of GM crops. Shops also need cover if genetically modified foods cause allergies or other ailments.

If, as some claim, GM crops and organic farming cannot exist side by side in such a small country, then the government should enter a genuine debate on which the public wants.

© Guardian Newspapers Limited 2001

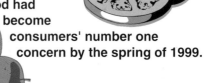

Public concern

Research undertaken by Mintel International measured the increase in public concern in Great Britain about GM food between August 1998 and April 1999. GM food had become consumers' number one concern by the spring of 1999.

Top five public concerns about food issues

Food issue	1998	1999
GM food	36%	47%
Pesticides in fruit and vegetables	42%	41%
BSE	37%	36%
Food poisoning	36%	32%
Use of antibiotics in meat	30%	31%

Base: 1518 adults (August 1998); 997 adults (April 1999). Respondents were able to choose up to 5 issues from a list of 18.

Source: Mintel International

The great food gamble

Information from Friends of the Earth

People's concerns about GM foods are deep-seated and long-standing. Food crises such as the BSE disaster have undermined the credibility of the scientific and regulatory establishment. Biotech companies and the regulatory authorities consistently claim that GM crops are safe to eat because they are subjected to a thorough and rigorous testing. This document outlines the system to which GM crops are subject and details the many gaps in understanding, technical expertise and procedure which exist. Indeed, so poor is the faith of regulators in their own systems that monitoring systems are being proposed in order to pick up health effects after GM crops have been approved for use in food. It is the conclusion of this report that the safety assessment process, as it stands, is not adequate to pick out every GM crop harmful to human or animal health.

The challenge of GM foods

There is a distinct difference between GM crops and those produced by traditional selection breeding. Selection breeding moves genes around within a species by crossing varieties together, genetic modification introduces genes from other species, even very distant ones. Whatever technique is used to insert novel genes, the genetic constructs are inserted at random into the host's genome. The imprecise and blunt genetic regulation mechanisms associated with novel genes contrast sharply with the tight and precise control of native genes. Finally, because of the expense of developing novel genetic constructs, the same novel genes are often inserted into many different crops, with the result that the same novel proteins are present in a wide range of foods.

Due to the uncertainties inherent in genetic modification, the effects on GM organisms are often undesired and unexpected.

Friends of the Earth

Documented effects include disruptions to the metabolism – alterations in the composition of GM crops have, in some cases, been observed for ones already on the market. Functional GM foods are being developed, such as vitamin A-producing rice, in which complicated genetic modifications aim to change the metabolism of the plant. This greatly increases the chances that unexpected changes in metabolism and composition will occur.

Substantial equivalence

The Royal Society of Canada recently reported that the use of substantial equivalence is 'scientifically unjustifiable'. Substantial equivalence is the concept which underpins the safety assessment of GM crops around the world. The basic premise is that if a GM food is shown by composition analysis to be the same as a non-GM food then it should be considered to be as safe as the non-GM food. However, GM foods cannot be exactly the same as non-GM foods, by the very fact of the novel proteins they contain, and so it was determined that they would be considered as safe as normal foods if they were substantially equivalent to them. However, there has never been any meaningful definition of 'substantially', and this has led to constant differences in interpretation. Interpretations of substantial equivalence vary around the world, meaning that GM crops may be deemed substantially equivalent in the US but not in the EU. These difficulties are likely to increase as GM crops become more complex.

Establishing the safety of GM foods

There is a large difference between our ability to create GM crops and

---

GM foods may be present in your food without your knowledge

Genetic engineering (GE), also known as genetic modification (GM), involves the artificial insertion of a gene from one species into another.

The technology has been in use for over 25 years but recently it has been applied to an increasing range of food crops for release into the environment.

Scientists have identified the effects that some specific genes have on an organism (e.g. which gene in a plant makes it resistant to a particular insect pest). However, many other side effects occur through different genes interacting with each other.

At present, these interactions are not well understood. Genetically modified organisms (GMOs) are commonly found in food products today, and often not labelled as such.

Consumer research has shown that 77% of the British public do not want GM crops grown in the UK (MORI) and 61% of the British public do not want to consume GMOs (MORI) but the large agrochemical companies are moving ahead, with the support of the government.

© Soil Association

foods, and our ability to test whether they are safe to eat. At present, examination of GM foods concentrates on simple chemical composition analyses. But this approach is criticised as being far too crude. It cannot detect unexpected or novel toxins as it focuses only on the known constituents of the food, and in many cases even the analysis of the levels of the known anti-nutrients is not done adequately, or at all. Understanding of the impact of food constituents is constantly changing, further hindering interpretation of observed results. New techniques for analysing GM foods, such as looking at genetic activity, total protein production and metabolic activity have been proposed but such techniques have not been applied to GM foods already on the market or in the pipeline.

Similarly, there are no established predictive tests to establish whether or not a novel protein may cause allergies. At present, companies rely heavily on theoretical assessments while the regulatory authorities have suggested monitoring for allergies after the food is released onto the market.

Animal tests have been used to support safety claims for GM foods and crops. However, the majority of these tests have been undertaken by biotech companies, and very few have been published or peer reviewed. In one case, the company has consistently refused to make public the detailed results of its studies. In another case, the same unpublished study was used to support GM crops produced by different companies. In a further case, when the company did make its research available for peer review, the study was severely criticised and the reviewers pronounced that in their opinion it was unfit for publication. Only a tiny number of safety assessments of GM foods have been published, and most remain unavailable to the public.

The US's guinea pigs
The US has the widest range of GM crops on the market and more than half of the US maize and soybean crops in 2000 were GM. Until May 2000, there was no statutory over-

sight of GM crops in the US, only a voluntary consultation procedure. More than 45 GM crops, containing at least 28 novel proteins, are listed by the Food and Drug Administration (FDA) as on the market. A number of applications for GM crops already marketed in the US have been severely criticised or rejected in the EU.

As there is no labelling of GM foods in the US, monitoring of health effects is impossible. Health effects might not become apparent immediately anyway, even if the authorities were attempting to monitor them. The case of allergic reactions reported after the consumption of products containing the GM maize Starlink was unusual simply because consumers were made aware that they were eating it. This is not usually the case, and so consumers would not be able to make any connection between health effects and GM food consumption – this means self-reporting is almost useless.

Conclusions
Enormous amounts of time and effort have been spent by governments and the biotech industry in presenting GM crops and foods as being well regulated and as safe as non-GM foods. Yet there are specific hazards which arise from GM foods distinct from those arising from non-GM foods. Firstly, there is the possibility, as a result of genetic modification, of significant alterations to the metabolism of GM food plants. Secondly, there is the fact that most novel proteins inserted into GM crops are entirely novel in the food chain, and that these are being placed into a wide range of food crops. The conclusion of this report is that the current system is unable to address these specific hazards satisfactorily.

Friends of the Earth believes the safety assessment of GM crops must be subjected to full review in light of the following:
- GM crops are not the same as those produced by traditional selection breeding, because of the random nature of genetic modification and the uncertainty of its consequences
- the ability to detect differences

in native genetic activity caused as a result of genetic modification, and understanding of their consequences, lags far behind the rate of development of GM crops
- difficulties in assessing the impacts of genetic modification will intensify as modifications become more complex.

Furthermore, Friends of the Earth believes the following procedures and practices are unacceptable:
- the presence of antibiotic resistance marker genes in a wide range of GM crops
- the use of substantial equivalence as a tool for assessing the safety of GM crops and foods
- the reliance on simple chemical analysis for examining the composition of GM crops and foods
- the reliance on theoretical analyses for establishing the allergenicity of novel proteins
- the use of inappropriate animal testing in support for the safety of GM crops and foods
- the withholding from public scrutiny of detailed safety assessments by biotech companies.

Friends of the Earth believes this system of oversight cannot guarantee the safety of GM products on the market. Gaps exist in regulatory procedures and their theoretical underpinnings, the information provided in support of GM crops, and the ability to test the safety of GM foods. It is frequently argued that there is no evidence that GM foods are any more dangerous than non-GM ones, and yet there is little credible scientific evidence to support this. It is possible that many GM foods are as safe as their conventional counterparts, but the system is not in place to make this judgement, nor is it adequate to detect any GM food that might be a long-term danger to consumers and farm animals.

- The above information is the Executive Summary of *The great food gamble – An assessment of genetically modified food safety*, produced by Friends of the Earth. See their web site on www.foe.co.uk for further details.

© Friends of the Earth

Genetically modified organisms (GMOs)

GMO questions and answers. Information from the National Farmers' Union (NFU)

Q: What is genetic modification?
A: It is a process that allows scientists to change plants or animals by identifying and inserting specific genes to promote desirable features like better flavour, resistance to disease and higher nutritional content.

Q: Is it ethical to manipulate the genes of a living organism?
A: In 1993, the Committee on the Ethics of Genetic Modification and Food Use, chaired by the Reverend Dr J. C. Polkinghorne, Master of Queens' College Cambridge, concluded that it was 'unable to accept the existence of a "moral taint" that would warrant a total ethical prohibition on genetically modified food use. A total ban would require the judgement that the whole process was morally defective.' The NFU shares this view while supporting the taking of precautions to protect animal welfare, and labelling to allow those who take a different stance to avoid genetically modified (GM) foods.

Q: What are the benefits of genetic modification?
A: There are many potential benefits.

In agriculture these include pest-resistant crops that reduce the need for pesticides with possible benefits for the environment; the ability to produce a more consistent supply of crops; food that is less affected by extremes of climate; lower production costs that mean lower retail prices; and better tasting food that stays fresher longer.

Q: Are GM crops grown in the UK?
A: They are not yet being grown commercially in the UK, though the Government and the European Union (EU) have already licensed some varieties and others are planned.

But food made from or containing GM products grown abroad is already on sale in the UK.

Q: What examples are there of GM food products?
A: Tomato purée using GM tomatoes and products containing GM soya are currently on the UK market. Another UK product is vegetarian cheese made using an enzyme produced by Genetically Modified Organisms (GMOs).

A variety of GM crops, including pest-resistant maize and cotton, and soya resistant to weed-killer, are being commercially grown in the USA, Canada and other countries. Work is also being carried out worldwide on products such as potatoes that contain more starch and less water so they take up less fat for frying.

Q: Are GM foods really necessary?
A: Genetic modification will produce plants or livestock with unique features that either cannot be developed or would take a long time to develop using current technology.

The regulated introduction of GM crops, engineered to complement local agricultural practices, will be one of the critical technologies used to boost food production to ensure the increasing world population is fed. The use of GMOs is already widespread in countries like China which urgently need to improve the diet and health of their population.

Q: Are there controls on the development and use of GMOs?
A: Yes. Several government departments have jurisdiction over GM crops and foods. They act on advice from committees such as the Advisory Committee on Novel Foods and Processes (ACNFP) and the Advisory Committee on Releases to the Environment (ACRE). Soon the Food Standards Agency will take over many responsibilities for controlling GMOs.

Q: Can GM crops cross with wild plants?
A: Yes, as is the case with non-genetically modified plants. The amount of outcrossing, when a plant breeds with another crop or weed, depends on the type of plant. For example, outcrossing of GM potatoes would be minimal but outcrossing of oilseed rape more likely.

Q: What are the possible long-term effects of GMOs?
A: The widespread growing of GM crops may cause environmental changes like those produced by the introduction of existing crops such as oilseed rape. The worst-case scenario would be herbicide-resistant weeds developing which could be more difficult to control. Research suggests this is unlikely to be a serious problem. However, the NFU supports the introduction of a lengthy post-release monitoring programme if, and when, GM crops are grown commercially in the UK.

In the meantime, there is ongoing research into the potential environmental effects of GMOs. The results are taken into account when the UK government and the EU make decisions on which crops should be authorised for growth.

Q: What does the NFU think about GMOs?
A: We believe genetic modification increases consumer choice and offers a range of benefits to agriculture and food manufacturing. But the NFU believes that GM crops are only acceptable if there is strict government licensing to ensure food safety and protect the environment, and with comprehensive labelling so that customers can choose whether or not they want to buy GM food.

The use of GMOs is already widespread in countries like China which urgently need to improve the diet and health of their population

---

The NFU has worked with the rest of the food chain to develop a preferred food labelling system. And a voluntary code of practice has been introduced to label foods containing GM soya and maize. The EU is currently revising its labelling requirements.

Q: What has the NFU done to advise its members on using GMOs?
A: The NFU and allied organisations have agreed on two codes of practice. They ensure that farmers are fully informed about GMOs enabling them to manage and store GM crops and products separately from conventional crops. A detailed report of the Biotechnology Working Group and various articles and documents have also been prepared as general information sources.

• The above information is from the National Farmers' Union's web site which can be found at www.nfu.org.uk

GM tomato could reduce cancer risk

By David Derbyshire, Science Correspondent

A genetically modified tomato that could help reduce the risk of cancer and heart disease has been created by British food scientists.

The fruit carries a gene normally found in petunias that gives its peel higher than normal levels of flavonols. These powerful antioxidants help mop up free radicals – destructive molecules that damage cells and hasten ageing.

Foods rich in flavonols include onions and tea. Tomatoes naturally have the compounds in their skin, but at far lower concentrations. The GM tomato skin had a 78-fold increase in flavonol levels, putting it on a par with onions, the team reports in *Nature Biotechnology*.

Taste was not affected, and 65 per cent of the flavonols were retained when the tomatoes were turned into paste. The scientists, led by Dr Martine Verhoeyen, from Unilever Research at Sharnbrook, Beds, said the research could lead to 'functional' tomato-based food products such as pizza.

One type of flavonol, quercetin glycoside, was 'significantly increased' in the peel of the modified tomatoes.

The risks

Information from the Food Commission

The Food Commission takes a sceptical view on the genetic modification of food crops. We have seen little benefit for consumers and increasing evidence of risks to the environment and possibly to our health. The problems include:

- Crops can be genetically engineered to withstand powerful weed-killing sprays. These GM herbicide tolerant crops can be sprayed as often as the farmer wishes, resulting in over-sprayed fields in which no wildlife can thrive.
- Crops can be genetically engineered to contain chemicals that poison insects. Whilst this may reduce crop losses it also decimates insect populations. Birds and animals which feed on these insects then die from lack of food.
- GM crops which are resistant to herbicides may interbreed with wild relatives to produce 'super-weeds' that will be difficult to control.
- GM crops encourage intensive mono-culture farming, reducing biodiversity and replacing the traditional British countryside with 'green deserts' of just one plant species.
- Animals which are genetically engineered to produce more meat can pay a high price. Pigs which have been genetically altered to produce extra growth hormones suffer from arthritis, gastric ulcers and diabetes.
- Allergic reactions. Up to two per cent of the population have allergic reactions to certain food types, such as milk, eggs, nuts, shellfish and cereals. When genes are transferred from one species to another these allergens can also accidentally be transferred, putting human health at risk. GM foods might also contain new allergens which could trigger allergic reactions in previously unsusceptible people.

THE

FOOD

COMMISSION

Publisher of the Food Magazine

- When we consume genetically modified food, the altered genetic material can cross through the gut wall and be absorbed into our blood and white blood cells, with unknown effects.
- Genetic engineering techniques include the use of antibiotic 'marker' genes which may increase the antibiotic resistance of dangerous bacteria. This could render our life-saving antibiotic medicines useless.
- Pollen from GM crops can travel many miles and can then pollinate organic or non-GM crops. Such crop contamination could mean whole fields of crops might have to be destroyed.

The Food Commission supports the call for a five-year freeze on putting any new genetically modified food into the shops or growing GM crops for commercial purposes in the UK.

The Food Commission

The Food Commission was set up in 1988 as the UK's first independent watchdog on food issues. It is a not-for-profit organisation and is funded by public donations and subscriptions.

Over the last 12 years our award-winning researchers have exposed the facts about modern food production and the secrets which the food industry prefers to keep hidden. Our independence from the government and food companies means that we can provide unbiased, accurate research which really helps people to eat a healthier diet.

If you would like to know more about our work and publications, including the *Food Magazine*, or would like to donate to our work, please write to us at the address below.

- The Food Commission, 94 White Lion Street, London N1 9PF. Tel: 020 7837 2250 Fax: 020 7837 1141. E-mail: foodcomm@compuserve.com Web site: www.foodcomm.org.uk

Biotechnology benefits

Information from Monsanto

Why biotechnology matters

Many people are beginning to appreciate more deeply the bonds between human well-being, social stability and the natural processes of earth that sustain all life. They are realising that the earth's capacity to continue providing clean air and water, productive soils and a rich diversity of plant and animal life is central to ensuring quality of life for ourselves and our descendants.

But current population growth is already straining the earth's resources. One of the few certainties of the future is that the world's population will nearly double, reaching almost 10 billion inhabitants by the year 2030. Humanity must respond to the growing pressures on the earth's natural resources to feed more people.

Biotechnology, which allows the transfer of a gene for a specific trait from one plant variety or species to another, is one important piece of the puzzle of sustainable development.

Experts assert that biotechnology innovations will triple crop yields without requiring any additional farmland, saving valuable rain forests and animal habitats. Other innovations can reduce or eliminate reliance on pesticides and herbicides that may contribute to environmental degradation. Still others will preserve precious groundsoils and water resources.

Most experts agree that the world doesn't have the luxury of waiting to act. By working now to put in place the technology and the infrastructure required to meet future food needs, we can feed the world for centuries to come and improve the quality of life for people worldwide.

'The current debate in Europe and the United States over genetically modified crops mostly ignores the concerns and needs of the developing world. Western consumers who do not face food shortages or nutritional

MONSANTO

deficiencies or work in fields are more likely to focus on food safety and the potential loss of biodiversity, while farming communities in developing countries are more likely to focus on potentially higher yields and greater nutritional value, and on the reduced need to spray pesticides that can damage soil and sicken farmers' (p. 3).

United Nations Human Development Report 2001

The benefits of biotechnology

The benefits of biotechnology, today and in the future, are nearly limitless.

Plant biotechnology offers the potential to produce crops that not only taste better but are also healthier.

The benefits of biotechnology, today and in the future, are nearly limitless

---

Agronomic or 'input' traits create value by giving plants the ability to do things that increase production or reduce the need for other inputs such as chemical pesticides or fertilisers. Our current products with input traits include potatoes, corn and soybeans that produce better yields with fewer

costly inputs through better control of pests and weeds. Already, farmers in Romania are growing potatoes that use 40% less chemical insecticides than would be possible using traditional techniques.

Quality traits – or 'output' traits – help create value for consumers by enhancing the quality of the food and fibre produced by the plant. Likely future offerings include potatoes that will absorb less oil when fried, corn and soya beans with an increased protein content, tomatoes with a fresher flavour and corn and sweet potatoes that contain high levels of amino acids, such as lysine.

Someday, seeds will become the ultimate energy-efficient, environmentally friendly production facilities that can manufacture products which are today made from nonrenewable resources. An oilseed rape plant, for example, could serve as a factory to add beta carotene to canola oil to alleviate the nutritional deficiency that causes night blindness.

'GM plants could nevertheless provide a means of significantly improving human health, first of all by supplying better quality food. Plants could be deprived of their most harmful ingredients (such as lipids which are bad for cholesterol) or enriched with molecules of nutritional benefit, the latter of particular benefit to southern countries. European laboratories recently developed a 'golden rice' enriched with carotene. This molecule is a precursor of vitamin A and could therefore help correct the nutritional deficiencies affecting millions of people. Another example is research aimed at increasing the lycopene content of tomatoes. This molecule has beneficial anti-oxidising effects which reduce the risk of prostate tumours.' http://europa.eu.int

See also 2001 report by Philippe Busquin, EU Research Commissioner, *GMO research in perspective.*

Growing 20 times faster, the GM oranges

Trees bear fruit in just a year

*By James Chapman,
Science Correspondent*

Growing oranges has always been a labour of love as farmers wait up to 20 years for trees to bear fruit.

But scientists have cut the process short by creating a tree that produces oranges within a year.

The superfast-growing fruits could soon be on supermarket shelves.

Spanish scientists, who developed the oranges using genetic modification, insist they are safe to eat. They hope the same process could be applied to other citrus crops.

But anti-GM campaigners condemned the development, claiming customers would be suspicious of oranges that had grown 20 times faster than usual.

Scientists from the National Institute for the Investigation of Agricultural and Food Technology in Madrid have been working on the trees for five years.

They altered the genetic structures of orange seeds by adding two genes from thale cress, a tiny flowering mustard plant found in many gardens.

'Citrus trees have a long juvenile phase that delays their reproductive development by between six and 20 years, depending on the species,' said the scientists' report in the journal *Nature Biotechnology*.

'With the aim of accelerating their flowering time, we transformed juvenile citrus seedlings to express genes which promote flower initiation.'

> *Orange varieties that would have taken years or decades to mature started bearing fruit almost immediately*

It worked. Scientists found the plants' juvenile phase was much shorter. Orange varieties that would have taken years or decades to mature started bearing fruit almost immediately.

Fertile flowers and fruits were produced 'as early as their first year', the scientists said.

'The fast-growing characteristics were inherited by the offspring of the genetically modified trees.

Because fruit and nut trees usually take so long to mature, harvesting is delayed and growers cannot quickly evaluate new strains. Genetic modification could change all that.

However, scientists admitted that when other researchers tried out the same process with hybrid aspen and poplar trees, the result was abnormal, infertile flowers only.

Pete Riley, a campaigner on GM food for Friends of the Earth, condemned the research.

'Apart from anything else, the European Union has capped orange production because there is such a surplus,' he said.

'And I can hardly see queues forming outside supermarkets for GM super oranges.

'The long-term effects on trees designed to produce fruit at a certain time must also be unknown at the moment. It's just another pointless piece of science from the biotech industry.'

*© The Daily Mail
March, 2001*

GREAT!! —YOU CAN TURN THE GENES OFF NOW...

Genetically modified food – key issues

Genetically modified organisms (GMOs) affect our lives and the environment in many ways

GM foods and human health

- Genetic modification has been associated with the creation of new toxins. A new disease occurred in the USA in 1989 which was eventually linked to a batch of the food supplement, Tryptophan, that had been produced through genetically modified organisms. Thirty-seven people died and one thousand, five hundred people were disabled as a result of eating the contaminated product. The exact nature of the link is still unsure as the US Food and Drug Administration was unable to come to any definite conclusions.
- If proper labels do not accompany genetically engineered products, allergy sufferers may no longer be able to tell what is safe for them to eat.
- Unexpected allergic reactions can be triggered (scientists proved that a brazil nut gene inserted into soya would result in people allergic to nuts suffering from an allergic reaction if they consumed the GM soya).
- There is a risk of increasing the incidence of antibiotic resistance in humans.
- Due to developments in this sort of food technology occurring only over the last few years, there has been little time to carry out sufficient long-term research to assess the health and safety implications to humans from ingesting genetically modified organisms.

GM foods and consumer choice

- Due to the current labelling legislation consumers will lose their right to choose whether or not to eat products that contain genetically modified ingredients.

- Products containing up to 1% of genetically modified ingredients will not need to be labelled as GM foods under current labelling directives.
- Religious groups lose their option of avoiding products that contain genes from certain animals (e.g. Muslims may unwittingly eat genes from a pig).
- No legislation exists to protect the crops of farmers who want to stay GM free from GM pollen, resulting in all crops being 'contaminated' over time.

GM crops and the environment

- Genetically modified material can be transferred to other crops and weeds but once released it is impossible to 'clean up' any unforeseen consequences. The Soil Association commissioned a report on the dispersal of maize pollen which has shown that pollination can occur at significant distances, threatening non-GM crops.
- Genetically modified plants which are designed to kill pests can kill beneficial insects as well. This also has a knock-on effect on birds who rely on insects in their diet.
- Plants modified for herbicide resistance will encourage increased usage of those agrochemical inputs and have a devastating effect on crop biodiversity. Herbicides kill a wide range of wild plants as well as insect, birds and other animals that depend on these plants for food and shelter.
- Genetically modified crops may have unpredictable effects on the ecological balance.
- Genetic modification to develop insect-resistant crops may encourage the development of resistance in insect populations.

© Soil Association

16

The case for crop biotechnology

What are the benefits of GM technology? What are the risks? Are the risks worth taking?

The case for crop biotechnology

The headlines about genetically modified (GM) food have been alarming and it wouldn't be surprising if you wanted nothing to do with it. There may be risks attached to GM technology, but we believe there are also enormous potential benefits – and that these benefits far outweigh the risks.

CropGen has been established to make a case for GM crops (crop biotechnology). Where we see real benefits we'll say so loudly. But if we have concerns we'll be just as vocal.

It's only possible to reach decisions about GM crops on reliable information and you can find the sources for the evidence we use, on our website (www.cropgen.org).

The barrage of criticism levelled at GM crops could well deny us many real benefits – benefits to the environment in terms of reduced use of chemicals, to the consumer in the form of more nutritious foods and to the developing world through a more secure supply of food.

At a time when people increasingly demand to know how technology affects them, any new development will have to work hard to gain public acceptance. That's no bad thing. More open debate about science and technology is long overdue but if crop biotechnology is sacrificed along the way it could be one of the great missed opportunities of our time.

CropGen is funded by, but operates independently of, the crop biotechnology industry. CropGen's panel of specialists answer some of the most frequently asked questions about crop biotechnology.

What exactly is a GM crop?

GM stands for genetic modification. A gene is an instruction and each of

our cells contains tens of thousands of these instructions. In humans, these instructions work together to determine everything from our eye colour to our risk of heart disease. The reason we all have slightly different characteristics, even from our brothers and sisters, is that before we are born our parents' genes get shuffled about at random.

Exactly the same principles apply to plants. If you're a gardener, you might save seed from a favourite plant, hoping you'll get another plant exactly the same. But because genes get shuffled about, you might get something that looks rather different. It's still the same kind of plant but it's bigger or smaller or a slightly different colour.

For thousands of years farmers have selected plants with the characteristics they want, such as extra seeds in a pod or the ability to survive in the cold. By crossing the best plants they hoped to produce even better varieties. But this approach is a bit like playing a fruit machine: you hit the jackpot only very occasionally. So since the 1950s, plant scientists have lent a hand.

Deliberately exposing seeds to radiation, for instance, increases the chance that one of them might produce a more useful plant. The barley variety Golden Promise was produced in this way and has been growing in Britain for 30 years.

Unlike these earlier methods, GM techniques allow specific genes to be copied into a plant. Because

the scientists know a great deal about the genes they're working with, it's easier for them to 'track' the genes, understand their effects and eliminate unwanted side effects long before the plants are used in field trials or grown commercially.

But surely it's wrong to interfere with nature like this?

Even with biotechnology, nature is still in charge. Genes can only be inserted into plants successfully if nature agrees. Otherwise the plant is unlikely to survive and certainly won't reproduce.

What are the benefits of GM crops?

GM technology can help to reduce the amount of chemicals used in agriculture. For example, making crops naturally resistant to a specific pest means that fewer insecticides are needed to get rid of that pest with little impact on beneficial insects. In the same way, if crops are made resistant to a particular herbicide, just one or two applications will be enough to control weeds in the field rather than having to use a number of different herbicides. (Currently, without the use of chemicals, we would lose about 40 per cent of our crops.)

In the future, GM crops will be able to provide foods with improved nutritional value, longer shelf-life and lower prices.

How can you tell what will happen when genes are inserted?

It's not possible to control the exact point within the plant's own genes where a copied gene is inserted. The gene's location is important because it affects how it will work. It may not work at all or it may affect other processes taking place in the plant. All of this is explored in the laboratory. Only after years of testing, when scientists are confident of their laboratory results, does a GM plant get to the field trial stage.

Compared with conventional methods, where thousands of genes are crossed at once, GM techniques are far more precise. In fact, conventional methods can and do sometimes go wrong. For instance, a potato bred in the conventional way in the 1950s contained more of its natural poisons than normal and killed several people. Because of the rigorous testing of GM crops, this would be spotted and the crop would be withdrawn at the laboratory stage.

Doesn't the GM industry put profits before safety?

It's clearly against any biotechnology company's interests to put profits before safety. What's more, no other crops are regulated or tested for safety to the same extent as GM crops. It's not because GM carries more risks but simply because people want additional assurances about new technology.

What about Monarch butterflies? Isn't there evidence to show that they have been adversely affected by GM crops?

This well-publicised laboratory experiment was designed to show what might happen in the worst imaginable situation. In the experiment, Monarch caterpillars were encouraged to eat high levels of pollen from GM maize containing a natural toxin called Bt (Monarch caterpillars would not normally choose to eat maize pollen in the wild). Unsurprisingly, some of the caterpillars died. The next question was: although they wouldn't choose to eat maize pollen, would the caterpillars be exposed to lethal levels of Bt toxin in the field? It was shown that Monarch caterpillars would almost never be exposed to such high levels of the toxin. Unfortunately, these results were not widely publicised. More information about this and other 'controversial' research is available on our web site.

Do GM crops affect diversity in the countryside?

Some GM crops have the potential to increase diversity by allowing more environmentally friendly practices compared with conventional farming methods. For example:

- In the USA, GM cotton uses up to 85% less insecticide than non-GM cotton. That's 85 per cent less insecticide to pollute rivers, leave residues in the soil and affect harmless insects.
- In the UK, results from GM sugar beet trials show that it can reduce total herbicide use by about 30 per cent. As a result weeds can be left for longer before they are controlled which is good for diversity because weeds are a source of food for insects and birds.

GM crops are already enabling farmers in other parts of the world to grow high quality crops with less environmental impact and more opportunities to encourage wildlife.

What effect do GM crops have on nearby plants?

It's true that pollen from GM crops may travel into neighbouring fields and come into contact with nearby plants and weeds. But only plants immediately next to a GM field are likely to be fertilised. Even then, this would only happen if the plants were

compatible and flowering at the same time.

The likelihood of fertilisation actually happening is assessed carefully by the Government's Advisory Committee on Releases to the Environment before any GM crop is allowed to be planted in the open. All GM traits will be tested extensively before their use is allowed in the UK.

Don't we run the risk of encouraging super-weeds and super-pests?

If farmers used herbicide-tolerant crops in isolation there probably would be some risk of tolerant weeds. But in reality farmers already rotate both crops and herbicides to minimise the chances of tolerance. So, with GM, farmers can still protect their crops but with fewer chemicals and with no added risk of tolerance.

Insect pests could become resistant to GM plants just as they do to insecticides. For this reason, where GM insect-resistant crops are grown, there are strict regulations, backed up by frequent inspections, to ensure that non-GM 'refuge areas' are established within the crops to reduce or prevent the development of resistance.

Aren't humans who eat genetically modified food at risk?

Before any GM foods are approved for sale in the UK they're tested rigorously by independent expert committees. These bodies approve a new GM food only when they're completely satisfied that it's as safe as its conventional counterpart. It's a similar story in other parts of the world, so it's not surprising that, in countries where millions of people have been eating GM foods for five years or more, there are no reports of adverse effects on health.

Also, there isn't any evidence that GM foods fed to animals do them any harm or harm the humans who eat them.

Aren't many people worried about new allergies?

New GM foods are tested exhaustively for possible allergic reactions. There's already an example of the effectiveness of this testing: an experimental GM soya variety contained a gene from Brazil nuts which made the soya potentially allergenic. This problem was identified, and the development of the soya stopped, long before it got anywhere near the marketplace. In the future GM may be used to produce non-allergenic nuts. And there's already research under way to produce non-allergenic rice.

There's also a concern about antibiotic resistance isn't there?

Antibiotic resistance is an extremely worrying problem. It's been caused by the overuse of antibiotics in both humans and animals and it became a major concern long before GM crops were planted.

Antibiotic resistance genes are sometimes used by researchers in the laboratory to help check whether the gene they are interested in has been successfully inserted. However, no one would consider using a critical human antibiotic resistance gene in a crop and neither would it be approved. The use of antibiotic resistant genes is convenient but not essential and alternative methods are well advanced.

Consumers have a right to know what's in their food, don't they?

Of course they do. In the UK, we already have the most comprehensive labelling regulations in the world. Retailers and manufacturers in Britain agreed to a voluntary labelling scheme for GM products several years ago. Tomato purée made from GM tomatoes was clearly labelled and sold very well. Since then, new EU regulations have come into force so that all food containing GM ingredients (over a one per cent threshold) has to be labelled.

What is CropGen?

CropGen is an initiative designed to give consumers and the media reliable information on the subject of GM crops (crop biotechnology). At its heart is a panel of independent scientists and other specialists, all of whom broadly believe that crop biotechnology has many potential benefits which are not being heard.

All panel members are experts in their field and are able to address the key issues relating to GM crops. None of the panel members is directly employed by any of the funding companies. The companies which fund CropGen cannot veto any of the panel's positions on any issue or interfere with its activities.

CropGen's mission

CropGen's mission is to make the case for crop biotechnology by helping to achieve a better balance in the debate about GM foods and crops in the UK. This article addresses only some of the main questions about crop biotechnology. If you want to know more, please visit our website: www.cropgen.org, or call our information line on 0845 602 1793 during normal office hours.

© CropGen

GM crops

Take a closer look

This Government's number one priority on all GM issues is to ensure the protection of the environment and human health.

No GM crops will be grown commercially in the UK until the Government is satisfied that there will be no unacceptable effects on the environment.

Why test GM crops?

Many people are concerned about the genetic changes to our plants that science has made possible, and many question whether we should be planting genetically modified (GM) crops in our fields.

The Government recognises these concerns, along with the potential benefits offered by GM technology. The UK is leading Europe in adopting a *precautionary* approach to looking at this new technology.

That is why carefully controlled and monitored tests of GM crops are essential.

Following years of tests in laboratories and on small plots of land, the GM crops now being tested in UK fields have already been confirmed as safe to human and

animal health. Direct effects on the surrounding environment have also been assessed by independent experts and confirmed as safe.

The Government has now set up the research Farm Scale Evaluations programme to examine whether there are any damaging environmental consequences from growing GM crops in larger fields. The weed control regimes associated with these particular types of GM crops will bring changes in farm management practices, and we need to check what that might mean for the environment. Only by growing the crops under the most normal farming conditions possible can real results be collected.

Farm Scale Evaluations – what are they all about?

Fields in England and Scotland, representing a wide range of current farming practices, are selected and planted with a GM crop in part of the field, of about 10 hectares (25 acres). The rest of the field is planted with an equivalent non-GM crop.

The crops to be used this year, which are each modified to be tolerant to certain types of weed killer, are:

- Fodder maize – which would be used in making silage;
- Oil seed rape – sown either in spring or autumn;
- Beet (both sugar beet and fodder beet).

The farmer looks after the crops using normal farming practices. The non-GM crop is treated with the usual range of weed and pest controls, and the GM crop is treated, if necessary, with the weed killer to which its modification has made it tolerant.

Research is being done by independent researchers – including world renowned experts in this area. During the growing season of the crops, they will count the number of weeds and insects, including bees and butterflies, in both the GM and the non-GM side of the field and in the field margins. The effects of any changes will be monitored closely. By doing this, we will be able to tell whether there are any differences in farmland wildlife between the GM and non-GM crop sides of the field. Researchers will also look at the pollen flow and cross-pollination as appropriate for these crops.

The research is being overseen by a Scientific Steering Committee – an independent body of scientific experts, including scientists from English Nature, RSPB and academia, set up to oversee the Evaluations.

To get enough evidence, the researchers must look at a total of around 60 to 75 fields treated in this way for each crop. This will be done over three years. All results will be made public.

This summer there will be up to 80 field sites in total.

Safety

Only GM crops that have been carefully assessed and are considered to be safe to human and animal health and which do not pose any direct environmental risks, are granted a licence, by either the UK or the European Union, to allow them to take part in the Evaluations.

The independent committee advising the Government on whether to release crops into the environment has already rigorously examined information about the crops themselves and their possible impact on the environment and human health.

Following years of tests in laboratories and on small plots of land, the GM crops now being tested in UK fields have already been confirmed as safe to human and animal health

---

These independent experts have advised that while none of the crops *in themselves* will harm any person or animal, more information is needed about the possible environmental impact of growing them in normal farming situations. This is why the Farm Scale Evaluations programme was developed.

The advisory committee has carefully considered the way in which the Evaluations will be carried out and have advised that, because the tests will be carefully controlled and regularly monitored, they do not present any risk to either the environment or to human health.

Indeed there are good reasons to suggest that these crops may reduce the environmental impact of weed control in agricultural crops, and the Government believes it is right to keep an open mind on the potential advantages or disadvantages these crops may offer.

Your questions answered

How can I trust the research?

- The Evaluations are being carried out by independent researchers, who will monitor the crops as they are being grown, and record and compile the results;
- Other independent scientists will be asked to check and review the results;

- You will be able to see the results of the Evaluations;
- There will be no commercial growing of GM crops until the Government is satisfied there will be no unacceptable impact on the environment.

No one wants GM crops, so why do we have to have the tests?

- The Government recognises that consumers want to be able to choose whether or not to buy goods which are genetically modified. It also recognises that scientists are developing this technology and will continue to do so, and that there may be benefits to be gained. The aim of the Farm Scale Evaluations is to ensure that the Government has enough information about the impact of these crops on the environment. This will ensure that any crops which come to the market are safe and will not have an unacceptable impact on the environment.

How can I find out more?

- Department of the Environment, Transport and the Regions (DETR) Web site; www.environment.detr.gov.uk/fse/index.htm
- Cabinet Office Web site; www.gm-info.gov.uk
- Come to one of the public meetings being held during the spring – details can be found on the DETR Web site;
- Or you can contact us direct at – GM Crops Policy, DETR, Zone 3/H10, Ashdown House, 123 Victoria Street, London SW1E 6DE. Telephone: 020-7944-3409 E-mail: biotech@detr.gsi.gov.uk You can get access to the Internet at your local library.

The Government has an open mind and is neither pro- nor anti-GM crops. It is pro-environment, pro-safety and pro-consumer choice.

- Department of the Environment, Transport and the Regions (DETR), Eland House, Bressenden Place, London SW1E 5DU. Telephone 020 7890 3000. Web site: www.detr.gov.uk

Is GE food safe?

Information from www.globalissues.org

Introduction

An issue that has entered the mainstream media in a lot of countries (noticeably not really in the US) is Genetic Engineering (GE) or Genetic Modification (GM) of food. A lot of food that we eat today contains genetically modified ingredients and usually without our knowledge.

Supporters of this technology maintain that it ensures and sustains food security around the world as the population increases.

As time goes on, the science behind genetic engineering is no doubt improving. While bio-technology could be the wave of the future and genetically modified foods could really provide alternatives to help increase food production, there is a growing wave of concern from citizens, farmers and scientists who question the way the research is currently being handled by a few large, profit-hungry corporations. That is, as well as scientific debates on the merits of genetically engineered food, there are equally, if not more important, debates on the socioeconomic ramifications of the way such science is marketed and used. Critics believe:

- The problem of food shortages is a political and economic problem.
- Food shortages and hunger are – and will be – experienced by the poorer nations.
- GE food is an expensive technology that the farmers of the developing nations would not be able to afford easily.
- Patenting laws go against the poor around the world and allow biotech companies to benefit from patenting indigenous knowledge often without consent.
- This is also a very young and untested technology and may not be the answer just yet.
- Crop uniformity, which the biotech firms are promoting, will reduce genetic diversity making them more vulnerable to disease

Some recent events

- Biotech industry promotes 'functional foods' as a second generation of GE foods.
- A new (but a bit weak) biosafety treaty will allow the regulation of transport and release of genetically modified organisms.
- Monsanto decide not to market terminator seeds for now.
- The world's two largest food production companies said that they will withdraw their acceptance of GE foods.

and pests. This furthers the need for pesticides, which are created by the same companies creating and promoting genetically engineered crops.

Hence this leads to questions of the motives of corporations and countries who are using the plight of the developing world as a marketing strategy to gain acceptance of GE food as well as dependency upon it via intellectual property rights. That they are against any labelling or other precautionary steps and measures that states may wish to take is of paramount concern.

The way in which we reach the answer to the question, 'are GE foods safe?' is where a lot of the problem lies. A quick acceptance of GE foods without proper testing etc. could show corporate profitability to be very influential, while a thorough

It may be that genetically modified food can benefit us, but we cannot know that at this time because much needed testing has not been done and current studies point to dangers rather than benefits

debate and sufficient public participation would ensure that real social and environmental concerns are in fact adhered to. And this pattern would probably indicate to us how other major issues in the future ought to be dealt with.

There is also the issue of do we actually need genetically engineered food, given that much third world agriculture in small biodiverse farms is actually very productive. It has been largely international and national politics and economics that have prevented food reaching hungry people, not a lack of production, and that have caused poverty that prevents people from being able to afford food in the first place.

Is it safe?

The potential benefits of genetically engineered food are exciting. At the same time though, there are real concerns on biodiversity, the eco-system and people's safety if such food has not been tested properly and guaranteed to be safe. As economics are factored in, there is also some concern as to who benefits from such technology, people in need, or people who need more.

No adequate testing

The reason that genetically engineered food could be dangerous is because there has been no adequate testing to ensure that extracting genes that perform an apparently useful function as part of that plant or animal is going to have the same effects if inserted into a totally unrelated species. It may be that in the long term, genetically modified food could provide us with benefits and be a safe alternative, but we cannot know that at this time due to the lack of safety testing.

The testing that has been done is often to ensure the crop grows. There has been less emphasis on testing the *effects* or testing the wider ecology and the associated impacts.

'It is often claimed that there have been no adverse consequences from over 500 field releases in the United States. In 1993, for the first time, the data from the U.S. Department of Agriculture (USDA) field trials were evaluated to see whether they supported these safety claims. The Union of Concerned Scientists (UCS), which conducted the evaluation, found that the data collected by the USDA on small-scale tests had little value for commercial risk-assessment. Many reports fail to mention – much less measure – environmental risks.'

Vandana Shiva, *Stolen Harvest* (South End Press, 2000), p.102

Bit different to the way nature works

'In industrial systems, time is money: speed is tied to efficiency because of competition and the need for returns on investments. The control and compression of time is central to the creation of profit. By contrast, in nature everything has its own time, rhythm and season. This natural time is a barrier to productivity and profit (Adam 1998).'

From the 'Politics of GM Food: Risk, Science and Public Trust' Special Briefing #5, ESRC Global Environmental Change Programme, University of Sussex and launched at the House of Commons, London, 18 October 1999.

Crossbreeding by farmers and evolution by nature has always involved gene transfer between similar species, not completely different species like a fish and a potato.

With the increasing drive for maximised productivity and profits, the diversity of crops used is being reduced. If the diversity is reduced enough the benefits that the diversity gives – resistance to disease, better ability to cope with environmental extremes, increased yields etc. – is also reduced.

Scientists have warned that non-target species can be affected by genetically modified food. They also urge a precautionary approach to allow science, law and regulations to catch up with the advances that have been made. Some GM crops still seem to require pesticide use as well.

Long-term effects are unknown

Even if there has been some testing, the long-term effects to humans, animals and the environment are unknown. The full ramifications of modified genes 'escaping' and mixing with unmodified ones are unknown.

It may be that genetically modified food can benefit us, but we cannot know that at this time because much needed testing has not been done and current studies point to dangers rather than benefits. However, a group of scientists in the UK do claim that GE food may be safe, but mention that the long-term effects are still unknown. (Also, note that a lot of field tests that companies do perform are aimed at assuring that their products are grown as expected, not always necessarily looking into wider effects.)

So why are they still being given the go-ahead?

- One reason is that there is a lot of money and profit involved in this.
- Another reason seems to be that in campaigns and referendums, a lot of emphasis is put on the fact that transgenic research-animals would help in the field of medicine and so distorts the purpose of the referendums that are usually about patent and food-related effects of genetic modifications.
- One potentially useful point for genetically engineered foods is that they should reduce the amount of pesticides that are used. However, pesticide usage has actually remained the same, or even increased, with the use of GE food. And the companies that make pesticides are the ones that also make GE food ingredients.
- The above information is from the web page www.globalissues.org/ EnvIssues/GEFood/ IsGEFoodSafe.asp The page provides links to other articles and news reports and is updated regularly

© Anup Shah

GM decision condemned by consumer groups

The Food Standards Agency's (FSA) decision not to support a key plank of proposed reforms to the GM labelling regime has been criticised by leading consumer groups in a joint letter to FSA Chairman, Sir John Krebs.

Consumer groups were hoping the FSA would support European proposals to extend and strengthen GM labelling laws. Instead, they have taken a step back through their decision not to support the labelling of GM derivatives (ingredients made from GM material but in which the modified DNA has been destroyed during processing).

Deirdre Hutton, National Consumer Council Chairman, said: 'We are very disappointed with the FSA's decision. Our own research found strong consumer support for GM labelling and over half of those surveyed want to know specifically about GM derivatives in the food they eat. The FSA claims that it would be difficult to enforce derivative labelling. But, that's not good enough. Just because some people drive too fast isn't an argument for not having a speed limit.'

Kim Lavely, Consumers' Association Deputy Director, said: 'The FSA has let down consumers on this occasion. The European Commission is proposing to strengthen and extend GM labelling in the interests of consumers but the FSA have voted for a much weaker option. We don't see how this fits with the FSA's supposed commitment to consumer choice and information.'

- The above information is from the National Consumer Council's web site which can be found at www.ncc.org.uk

© National Consumer Council, 01/10/01

GM foods affect your life

Here are some things you should know . . .

If you worry about food safety you should know that GM foods are as safe as other foods and that GM crops are grown with fewer pesticide applications than traditional crops.

If you treasure butterflies you need to know that pesticides used in conventional farming are far worse than GM crops for butterflies.

If you have allergies you need to know that GM technology can eliminate food allergens and that all GM crops are extensively tested to make sure that no new allergens are introduced. In addition, GM crops are being created in which the major allergens have been eliminated.

If you are worried about cancer you should take note of the fact that 99.99 per cent of the carcinogens in your food supply are natural chemicals that humans have been eating for thousands of years. However, GM technology provides the means of increasing levels of phytoestrogens, isaflavones, carotenoids, and other antioxidants known to prevent cancer.

If you are a woman and worried about getting sufficient iron you should know that genetic modification can increase the iron content of cereals and has eliminated chemicals (phytic acid) that prevent iron absorption.

If you have doubts about the government's approval of GM crops you need to know that extensive testing and a long approval process accompany every GM crop introduction. In the United States, three agencies regulate these crops.

If you care about the environment you may want to know that GM foods can make a significant contribution to alleviating the negative impact that agriculture has on our environment.

What is a gene?

Genes are the units of inheritance first discovered in the middle of the nineteenth century by Gregor Mendel. He examined thousands of pea plants and discovered that some pea flowers had a purple colour that was inherited when peas were crossed. Now we know that genes are made of DNA and are arranged in long strings on the cell's chromosomes. Bacterial cells have about 2,000 different genes, a flowering plant has some 25,000 genes, and humans may have as many as 50,000. Every cell has two copies of every gene. Each gene has the information to make a specific protein. Thus, in peas the gene for 'purple' specifies a protein that converts a colourless chemical into a purple pigment in the pea flower. When the gene is passed from one generation to the next, so is the capacity to make the purple pigment.

If you are worried about eating genes you should know that a GM-free meal that has ten ingredients (wheat, potato, broccoli, meat, etc.)

GM foods can make a significant contribution to alleviating the negative impact that agriculture has on our environment

---

has billions of copies of 250,000 different genes. If five of those ingredients are GM crops you will eat an additional ten to fifteen genes. All those genes are quite readily digested by your stomach juices.

If you have religious beliefs you should be aware that ethicists and religious leaders do not object to genetic engineering of crops on ethical or religious grounds.

If you care about developing countries you should take note of the fact that the most eminent plant breeders in those countries want to have access to GM technology to breed more productive and more nutritious crops.

If you don't trust industry spokespersons then listen to independent university scientists. The overwhelming majority agree that GM technology is safe for the consumer and the environment and that it is needed to raise crop productivity. They also support scientific testing and regulation of such crops.

• The above information is from the San Diego Center for Molecular Agriculture (SDCMA) whose web site can be found at www.sdcma.org

Food production: old and new

Information from the John Innes Centre

JOHN INNES CENTRE

Introduction

Picture food – what comes to mind? Apples, carrots, bread, pizzas, chocolate? All these – whether raw, semi-processed or highly processed – are food. Because we all have to eat to survive, and because food is so important to health, what can be sold for human consumption is closely regulated. The word 'food' as used in the food industry therefore has strict meaning – perhaps surprisingly, it also includes drinks, any substance used in the production of food, and even chewing gum.

Biotechnology has already benefited the food industry; it has given us high-quality foods that are tasty, nutritious, convenient and safe. As research continues, it seems inevitable that biotechnology will have an increasing impact on the food we eat. It offers huge potential for increasing the range and quality of food available to us, particularly more nutritious, palatable and stable food. It also seems likely that it will continue to bring advantages to the processing and safety monitoring of our food supply.

Food processing

There is an increasing desire among many consumers for food to be as 'natural' as possible, because such food is perceived by consumers to be more nutritious and safer to eat. However, food processing preserves food that would otherwise perish and gives us an interesting and varied choice of products. Most food nowadays undergoes some form of processing. In fact, it has been estimated that more than 80% of food sold in the UK is processed. What's more, food processing has been going on for centuries – and so too has the use of biotechnology in food processing.

Traditional biotechnology

There cannot be many people who haven't consumed bread, wine, yoghurt or cheese. These products, like many others including salami, pickles, soy sauce, vinegar, beer and cider, are made using the natural processes of living organisms (e.g. fermentation), in other words, using biotechnology.

Such 'traditional' biotechnology has played an important role in the development of our food supplies for thousands of years. Biotechnology was practised by our ancestors in an effort to find new ways of producing foods. Through trial and error, they learned how to breed and domesticate animals, and developed a variety of food crops. They also developed techniques, such as baking, brewing and fermentation, to process and preserve raw foods. Some traditional biotechnology techniques (such as the production of mycoprotein Quorn™ as an alternative to meat) have been developed much more recently. Nevertheless, such conventional techniques are widely accepted and generally do not cause public concern.

Modern biotechnology

'Modern' biotechnology, in contrast with 'traditional' biotechnology, also uses the techniques of genetic modification – the joining of pieces of genetic material (DNA) in new combinations. This allows characteristics to be transferred between organisms, to give new combinations of genes and improved varieties of plants or microorganisms for use in agriculture and industry. Some consumers are concerned about the safety of using the techniques of modern biotechnology.

How is modern biotechnology being used in the food industry?

The techniques of modern biotechnology are becoming an increasingly important part of the overall effort to improve methods of food production and to increase the variety and quality of foods. Modern biotechnology has potential applications in the production of food, food processing, and also in the assurance of food quality and safety.

What's available in the supermarket?

Although many genetically modified food crops are under development, very few have so far reached the supermarket shelf. The first genetically modified whole food to reach the shops was the FLAVR SAVR™ tomato in the USA, and the first product in the UK was tomato purée.

The recent introduction of genetically modified soybean has caused controversy. Up to 60% of processed foods contain soy or soy derivatives, such as starch, protein or oils.

Modern biotechnology is also being used to improve micro-organisms, processing aids (e.g. enzymes) or ingredients for use in the production and processing of food. The enzyme chymosin, which is used in the manufacture of 'vegetarian cheese', is an example of this type of genetically modified product.

• The above information is from the John Innes Centre's web site page www.jic.bbsrc.ac.uk/exhibitions/bio-future/fbtm.htm

© John Innes Centre, Norwich, UK.

Questions and answers

Genetically modified foods

What are genetically modified foods?
GM food is produced when one or more genes from a plant or animal are added or replaced with genes from another plant or animal. A gene may be 'piggy-backed' onto a virus which is then used to infect a plant or animal or it can be blasted using a 'gene gun'. These technologies enable scientists to create new 'modified' life forms, such as crops that are resistant to herbicide or tomatoes which rot more slowly.

Don't we have people to oversee the safety of GM foods?
In the UK, the Advisory Committee on Novel Foods and Products (ACNFP) considers applications from companies who want to sell genetically modified foodstuffs. Recent scrutiny has revealed that, on the ACNFP's sub-committees responsible for the licensing of food products, more than half of the advisers had interests in the GM food industry either through investments or employers. Overall, at least 13 can be directly linked to one of the three biggest players in the GM foods industry – Monsanto, Novartis and Zeneca. It should be remembered that although this committee plays an 'advisory' role, ministers cannot license products without their prior backing.

The committee evaluates food-stuffs – using data supplied by the actual companies who stand to profit. Much of this data comes from feeding trials using animals.

As a result of the publicity surrounding the safety of GM foods,

any company wishing to market a new food for human consumption is likely to feel under increasing pressure to provide more data showing no harmful effects. Part of this is almost bound to mean a massive increase in the use of animals.

But don't we need animal tests to find out if GM foods are safe for humans to eat?
Animal experiments for GM foods have obvious and inherent limitations:

Species difference – the simple fact is that different species can react differently to different substances. What if GM food adversely affected

> *It is fairly obvious that animals do not live as long as humans. Therefore, how can animals be used to determine any long-term health consequences in humans in order to establish the safety of GM foods?*

human memory, taste or ability to see colour? Animal experiments would be unable to pick up such reactions.

Animals such as rats have completely different dietary requirements to humans – to test GM food, animals will be eating totally inappropriate substances. The effect of forcing an inappropriate, alien diet on them can be so harmful to make even control groups ill, rendering any results meaningless. The sheer quantity of a GM substance that an animal will be forced to eat to measure toxicity also makes such experiments ridiculous. An example is the experiment conducted by Dr Pusztails at the Rowett Institute in Aberdeen, which involved rats being fed large quantities of raw and cooked genetically modified potatoes. This resulted in damage to their immune systems. The outcome sparked a great deal of controversy, but does anyone really believe that this experiment bears any relevance to humans?

Animals do not have the same life expectancy as humans – it is fairly obvious that animals do not live as long as humans. Therefore, how can animals be used to determine any long-term health consequences in humans in order to establish the safety of GM foods?

Animal experiments cannot predict allergic reactions in humans – allergens are a major concern surrounding GM foods. Genetic engineering routinely moves proteins into the food supply from organisms which would never have been consumed as food products. Virtually all known food allergens are proteins, which can trigger allergic reactions in some people. The USA has already seen a 50% increase in allergies to soya – a common ingredient used in 60% of processed foods – in the past year. This reaction was not predicted in animal tests.

Environmental factors – animal experiments are flawed because laboratory conditions are not the real world. Laboratory animals are extremely stressed, and genetically pure from in-breeding. Therefore, animal tests cannot predict the safety – or dangers – of GM foods for humans as a result of the unnatural environment in which the tests take place.

All of these factors have the potential to affect results significantly and render them meaningless. None of these warnings are heeded by the vested interests of the biotech companies, who claim GM foods to be safe on the basis of laboratory animal studies.

What about Third World hunger . . . won't GM foods help alleviate suffering?

According to the United Nations World Food Programme, the world

---

Genetic engineering is already a fact of life and death. It is not just animals but we who have become the 'guinea pigs' in a massive experiment

---

produces 1.5 times the amount of food needed to provide the world population with an adequate, nutritious diet. The reality is that it is the world's meat-eating habit that has resulted in Third World hunger. Deriving food from animals is an inefficient use of cheap and plentiful vegetable crops. It takes roughly 4kg of grain to produce 1kg of pork and 3kg to produce every kg of eggs. Therefore, there is not a problem with the quantity of food we can produce, it is access.

Anyway, claims that GM plants will produce more abundant crops has been refuted by the US Department of Agriculture. Experts found no increase in yields from crops in 12 of 18 areas. Farmers in 7 of the 12 areas even needed to use the same amount of pesticides as those growing

traditional crops. The GM companies have shown little interest in millet, cassava and sorghum crops – the staple diet of the world's poor. They prefer to concentrate on high value crops like tomatoes, cotton, oilseed and rape.

As public concern over the issue grows, calls have been made for more experiments on animals to demonstrate the harmlessness or otherwise of GM foods. Animal Aid believe that such experiments will only cause suffering to thousands of animals and confuse the GM debate even further by bringing forth more irrelevant results.

Genetic engineering is already a fact of life and death. It is not just animals but we who have become the 'guinea pigs' in a massive experiment, the consequences of which are not yet known. Like it or not, we are already eating GM foods in our everyday life, the consequences of which the biotech industry will never be able to recreate inside a laboratory.

• The above information is an extract from an Animal Aid factsheet. See page 41 for their address details.

© Animal Aid

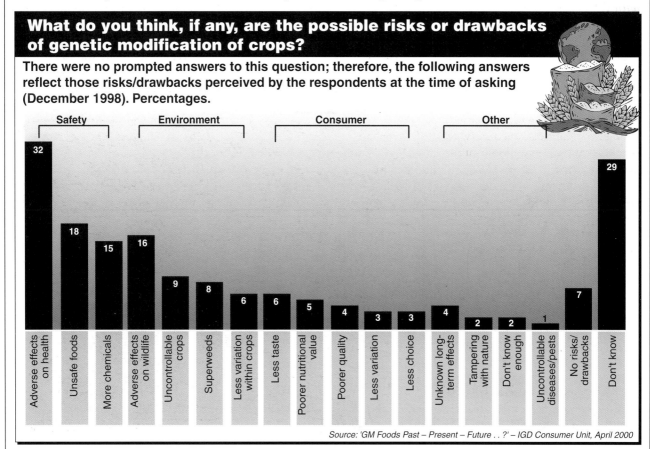

What do you think, if any, are the possible risks or drawbacks of genetic modification of crops?

There were no prompted answers to this question; therefore, the following answers reflect those risks/drawbacks perceived by the respondents at the time of asking (December 1998). Percentages.

Safety			Environment			Consumer					Other					
32	18	15	16	9	8	6	6	5	4	3	3	4	2	2	1	7	29
Adverse effects on health	Unsafe foods	More chemicals	Adverse effects on wildlife	Uncontrollable crops	Superweeds	Less variation within crops	Less taste	Poorer nutritional value	Poorer quality	Less variation	Less choice	Unknown long-term effects	Tampering with nature	Don't know enough	Uncontrollable diseases/pests	No risks/ drawbacks	Don't know

Source: 'GM Foods Past – Present – Future . . ?' – IGD Consumer Unit, April 2000

Why do we need them?

Grassroots gets to the root of a key issue, asking the people most closely involved what's *really* going on. Ruth Evans asks Patrick Holden of the Soil Association about genetically modified foods

The recent concerns over food security, ranging from BSE to genetically modified foods in the UK, mark a watershed in public awareness in two key areas; the link between food quality and health and the potential of consumer power to maintain the right to choose what we eat. It appears more and more people are making a conscious choice to buy non-genetically modified foods, with an increasing number buying organic as the only food supply credited to be free of genetically modified ingredients.

I asked Patrick Holden, Director of the Soil Association (founded in 1946 to promote organic farming), to clarify the most frequently asked questions surrounding genetically modified foods.

Q. All foods have been modified to some extent, so what's the difference with GM foods?
A. Genetic engineering differs from 'traditional' methods of cross breeding since genes are transferred between differing species rather than between the same species. In nature two different species cannot cross breed, concern lies with the natural equilibrium being disturbed and with the fact that the consequences are as yet unforeseen.

Q. There are no proven risks to health, the campaign against the introduction of GM foods has been regarded by its promoters as scaremongering.
A. Again it's the unforeseen effects which are the real threat. GM foods could pose a risk to the immune system as found by Stanley Ewan, a senior pathologist at the Aberdeen University Medical School, in his research on rats, developing brain disorders as a result of being fed GM potatoes. There is not enough research being done on the effects of GM foods, as in the case of BSE,

Green Direct

symptoms were being recorded years before the evidence started to appear. At the very least, the approach should follow the precautionary principle and delay until in-depth research has been carried out.

Q. It begs the question why we need GM foods in the UK in the first place, who's going to benefit, the multi-national companies, the supermarkets or the consumer?
A. The only group to benefit from GM foods are the multi-national companies. The consumer is robbed of choice and there is no evidence that GM foods will prove cheaper.

Q. What's the threat to the environment? Is there evidence for this claim?
A. Yes, there is clear and increasing evidence here that pollution of crops

from GM seeds has taken place and poses a real threat to biodiversity. The result of which is infertile herbicide-tolerant modified crops and the choice for organic taken away at one fell swoop. In a rapidly urbanised world, agriculture has become key to the future survival of the nation's biodiversity.

Q. Regarding the cross-pollination argument; how can GM crops pollinate with organic and other seed crops since they're supposed to be sterile and therefore unable to fertilise the following year like our 'normal' seeds?
A. GM crops can cross pollinate with non-GM and organic seeds. It is the terminator gene currently being formulated in the USA which is being bred to be sterile (where the seeds cannot be sown the following season), forcing farmers to buy seeds year after year from the large seed companies such as Monsanto. There is talk regarding creating buffer zones between GM crops and organic to avoid cross pollination which in effect means a land separation of

OUR POTENTIAL CUSTOMERS VALUE BIODIVERSITY HIGHLY...

- WELL, GET ONTO OUR LAWYERS AND PATENT IT !!

SURVEY

between 6 and 200 metres. How can this be a good enough buffer to protect organic crops against risk of pollination since the success or failure of the boundary depends on the direction of the wind?

Q. Aren't GM foods the answer to world hunger?
A. There is no evidence that genetic engineering can play a major part in feeding the world. The food shortage is not only about increasing yields – insect and herbicide tolerance and high and low management input are also major factors.

Q. What about claims that GM foods can potentially help tackle disease in developing countries, by transporting vaccines via modified fruits such as the banana?
A. This is mass medication via GM plants. The immune systems of crops will degrade once they are modified in this way. Basically you are tricking the plant to accept a foreign host and resist disease, producing plants containing an inadequate balance of nutrients.

Q. Haven't the House of Commons and the House of Lords banned GM foods in their canteen?
A. There is no official ban, although I suspect if one talked to the MPs many seek to avoid eating it.

Q. Will the new legislation on labelling GM ingredients in all foods suffice in terms of weeding out all GM ingredients and providing the consumer with a real choice?
A. The labelling directive requires companies to list GM ingredients in their food products, however ingredients containing approximately less than 2% of GM products are not required to be labelled and therefore go undetected. Tesco, Sainsbury's and Safeway, however, claim all their food products containing GM ingredients will be clearly labelled including derivatives of GM foods such as soya maize and cooking oil.

• The above information is an extract from *Grassroots*, the magazine produced by Green Direct. See their web site at www.greendirect.co.uk
© *Green Direct*

Supermarkets

What are the major supermarkets doing to get GM out of the food/feed chain?

Marks and Spencer
All fresh beef, lamb, pork, chicken, salmon (fresh and smoked), eggs and milk (England only) are from animals reared on a non-GM diet.
They are committed to working towards being able to offer customers the same assurances on all dairy products.

Iceland
All fresh chicken, chicken portions and chicken products are from animals fed on a non-GM diet. All meat is reared on a non-GM diet during the 'finishing phase'.
They are aiming to rear all livestock on non-GM diet throughout life, target dates are 2001 for pork, 2002 for lamb and 2003 for beef. They are working on a policy for dairy livestock.

Tesco
Will be non-GM in fresh poultry, eggs, fish and pork by June 2001 and in fresh sausage meat and bacon by September and October 2001 respectively.
They are 'talking to suppliers of other meat and dairy products to develop similar arrangements'.

Asda
A range of non-GM fed fresh chicken and eggs will be available from summer 2001 and a range of non-GM fed pork from autumn 2001.
'Asda is committed to removing GM from animal feed.'

Co-op
All fresh and frozen chickens, chicken portions, further processed chickens (e.g. chicken kiev) and free range eggs are fed on non-GM diets.
The Co-op has asked all their 'suppliers of meat, poultry and milk to put in place plans to ensure that no Co-op Brand product is derived from animals fed upon a diet containing GM crops'.

Safeway
Have made it clear to all their suppliers that they ' . . . wish to achieve non-GM status for animal feed as soon as possible'.
For chicken, pork, eggs and fish they expect to achieve non-GM status 'in the relatively near future'. For beef and dairy 'the infrastructure of feed management is too complex to make non-GM status achievable in the near future'.

Waitrose
All fresh British chicken is fed non-GM diets. Waitrose has not set a date yet for elimination of GM crops in animal feed but 'all efforts are being made to ensure this project is completed as soon as practicably possible'.

Sainsbury's
All fresh poultry will be sourced from non-GM feed by June 2001.
'Sainsbury's is committed to the removal of GM from animal feed and are progressively working towards its removal for own label animal products.'

Morrisons
Have made no commitment to going non-GM in animal feed.

Somerfield/Kwiksave
Have made no commitment to going non-GM in animal feed.

• The above information is an extract from Greenpeace's web site which can be found at www.greenpeace.org.uk
© *Greenpeace*

Biotech primer

As a life sciences company, Monsanto is a leading proponent of modern biotechnology in order to improve food, health and the environment. We are interested in taking positive steps to engage other interested parties in dialogue about agricultural biotechnology so that it can become better understood and appreciated by the public. With this in mind, we want to answer some common questions and concerns regarding biotechnology.

Why do we need this technology?

Demand for food is increasing dramatically as the world's population grows. Biotechnology provides us with a way of meeting this growing demand without placing even greater pressure on our scarce resources. It allows us to grow better quality crops with higher yields while at the same time sustaining and protecting the environment. It can also help to improve the nutritional value of the crops which are grown.

What is genetic modification?

Genetic modification is an accurate and effective way of achieving more desirable characteristics in plants without the trial and error of traditional methods of selective breeding.

For centuries farmers and gardeners have attempted to alter and improve the plants they grow. In the past this was done by cross-breeding one plant or flower with another in the hope of producing a plant with particular qualities such as a larger flower or a sweeter fruit. The processes used in the past attempted to bring about changes in plants by combining all the characteristics of one plant with those of another.

But as our understanding of plant life has grown, scientists have found ways of speeding up this process and making it more precise and reliable. It is now possible to identify exactly which genes are responsible

MONSANTO

for which traits. Using this information, scientists can make small and specific changes to a plant without affecting it in other ways.

An example of this is a potato which has been genetically modified to give it a built-in resistance to the Colorado beetle, which can destroy potato crops, thus reducing the need for chemical pesticides.

What sort of changes can be brought about by genetic modification?

Plants can be modified to bring about many types of changes which can be of benefit to consumers, the food industry, farmers and people in the developing world. Genetic modification can also contribute towards a more sustainable form of agriculture and bring environmental benefits.

- Fruit and vegetables can be modified to improve their taste and appearance. This means being able to provide consumers with the consistently high quality fresh produce they demand.
- Improvements can be made to the nutritional qualities of certain plants. For example, oil seed, from which some cooking oils are made, can be developed so that the oil has a reduced saturated fat content.
- Products can be modified in ways which will make it easier and cheaper to process them. For example, the modification of tomatoes to delay ripening has led to cheaper tomato purée.
- Plants can be modified to increase their ability to fight insects, disease and weeds, all of which can destroy or seriously damage crops. This not only increases the yield of these crops, but also reduces the need for pesticides.

- Plants can be modified to be resistant to drought or to grow in difficult conditions. This will have many benefits for parts of the world where the demand for food is increasing significantly and there is not enough good arable land.

How can we assure that these new developments are safe?

It is important that consumers feel confident about the food they buy. Modern biotechnology is therefore subject to strict controls.

These are designed to ensure that new genetically modified products are safe to eat and that they pose no new risks to the environment.

European legislation on novel foods is implemented in the UK by a strict regulatory process involving a number of different committees, each composed of independent experts. Many of these people are scientists but the committees also include individuals who are primarily concerned with ethical and consumer issues.

How do we know that genetically modified crops are safe to eat?

Background

Before any GM crops can be sown, or food produced from GM crops can be sold, they must go through a rigorous approval process, involving several expert committees.

The main committees responsible for food safety aspects of GM crops in the UK are:
- The Advisory Committee on Novel Foods and Processes (ACNFP)
- The Committee on Toxicity of Chemicals in Foods, Consumer Products and the Environment (COT)
- The Food Advisory Committee (FAC)

These food safety bodies are now controlled by the Food Standards Agency (FSA).

Transparency
In order to ensure transparency and accountability, the proceedings of all of these committees are available to the public, and they also hold public meetings.

What tests are done?
The food safety assessment carried out by the ACNFP requires biotechnology companies like Monsanto to submit genetically modified crops for extensive independent studies. These include:

- 'Mechanism of Action' test: A study to understand precisely what the added protein that has been inserted into the plant is intended to do. This is critical as it shows whether the protein added will cause any harmful effects (such as the production of toxic chemicals)
- A digestibility study – to establish, for example, how quickly the added protein is broken down inside the gut (in the case of GM soya, for example, this is around 60 seconds)
- A study to screen for known allergens and toxins (called 'Bioinformatics Screening')
- An acute oral toxicity study – comprising a two-week toxicology study in which the additional protein is fed in its pure form to mice, at a rate at least 1000 times higher than a human would ever be exposed to.
- Nutritional (wholesomeness) animal feeding studies – to establish that the new variety, for example GM soya, is equivalent in its composition, nutrition and functionality to non-GM soya
- Non-target animal studies – for pesticidal proteins only. (These studies involve extensive eco-toxicological evaluations based on testing both pure protein and/or the GM plant for toxic effects and desirable insects and/or animals that are important in the eco-system)

Where the above studies reveal that there are unique or unresolved issues concerning the added protein, the regulatory authorities can demand that further studies are carried out. These can include:

- Sub-chronic animal feeding studies – comprising medium-term feeding studies in animals, including chickens, ruminants and mono-gastrics
- Case-specific in vitro (i.e. outside a living organism) toxicology studies
- Further studies of the 'Mechanism of Action' of the protein
- In vivo (i.e. inside a living organism) protein fate studies
- Human clinical trials (e.g. food allergy evaluations) – though these tests are rarely required because of the extensive evidence which results from the other tests

What about the impact of genetically modified crops on the environment?
Genetically modified organisms may not be released into the environment without approval. In the UK, the environmental aspects of new foods are regulated through an EU directive. Initial laboratory work is controlled by the Health and Safety Executive (HSE) who consult the Advisory Committee on Genetic Modification (ACGM). Advice on the development of these crops is given to the government by a scientific committee, the Advisory Committee on Releases to the Environment (ACRE).

Many hundreds of field trials have been approved in the UK. Before approval for these trials can be given, a strict environmental risk assessment must be carried out under the auspices of the Department of Environment, Food and Rural Affairs (DEFRA), and approval has to be given by the Secretary of State. Approval to grow the crops commercially will not be given until the trials have been completed and the regulators are satisfied.

In other parts of the world, such as Canada and the USA, genetically modified crops are now grown extensively after the regulatory authorities there concluded that there was no threat to the environment. Many thousands of field trials with genetically modified crops have taken place worldwide since 1987 and by 2001 commercially grown plants covered an area in excess of 100 million acres.(www.isaaa.org)

Could the new genes in these crops be passed on to other plants?
The question of the transfer of genes from genetically modified crops to other plants is considered carefully by the regulators. They have accepted that there is no greater risk of this happening than exists with the conventional crops grown in this country at present. Our extensive experience of genetically modified crops which are grown elsewhere in the world supports this view.

Is Monsanto involved in commercial genetics other than food bio-technology?
Monsanto is currently involved only in agricultural biotechnology. This includes techniques for the transfer of genetic material or characters between plant species or between micro-organisms and plants.

Such developments are generally regarded as an extension of plant breeding, but they allow more precise transfer of single traits or characters than the more random nature of cross-pollination.

We are not at present involved in any work with human genetics or with human genes. Nor are we involved in work with animal genetics in relation to animal breeding.

What is Monsanto's overall safety and environmental record?
Monsanto has an exemplary safety and environmental record, and we also have a policy of openly publishing our performance in these areas. We produce an *Environmental Annual Review*, in which we publish full details of our emissions and programmes to reduce them, as well as employee health and safety data.

In the 1980s we began a programme to reduce air emissions by 90 per cent, a goal we achieved in

1992. Since then we have set new targets for further reductions in all emissions by 70 per cent, with an ultimate goal of 'zero impact'.

What about consumer information?
Labelling helps consumers decide what they buy. Decisions about the labelling of foods containing ingredients from genetically modified crops are made by the European Union, and the UK food industry began labelling many of these foods voluntarily in November 1997.

In order to help improve public understanding of modern bio-technology and genetic modifica-tion, the food industry in this country is working to keep consumers better informed. Public information is a priority and we at Monsanto are working to achieve this through a variety of different approaches.

• The above information is an extract from Monsanto's web site which can be found at www.monsanto.co.uk Alternatively, see page 41 for their address details.

Genetic modifcation of major crops

Summary of current developments

	Crop	Modifications
	Apples	Insect and disease resistance
	Brassicas	Pest resistance
	Coffee	Decaffeination
	Maize (corn)	Insect resistance, herbicide tolerance
	Melon	Slow ripening
	Oilseed rape (canola)	Herbicide tolerance, modified oil composition
	Papaya	Virus resistance
	Potato	Insect and virus resistance, higher starch content
	Raspberries	Virus resistance, slow ripening
	Rice	Increased iron and Vitamin A
	Salad crops	Herbicide tolerance, insect resistance
	Soya bean	Herbicide tolerance, virus resistance, modified oil composition
	Sugar beet	Herbicide tolerance, virus resistance
	Sunflower	Modified oil composition
	Sweet potatoes	Virus resistant
	Tomato	Increased antioxidants
	Wheat	Herbicide tolerance, modified starch types

Source: The Food Commission

Genes in the spotlight

Information from the European Food Information Council (EUFIC)

A recent UK public consultation[1] on developments in the bio-sciences found that while most people's associations with the word 'gene' were correct, some people were confused over the function of genes and some did not realise that they are consumed every day as part of our normal diet.

However, genes are found in almost every cell of all plants and animals. They are the units of inheritance, composed of DNA, which are transmitted from parents to offspring during reproduction. It is the genes, typically several hundreds of thousands for a particular species, which carry the information needed by the cell to create the numerous proteins that the organism needs to develop, grow and multiply.

Consequently, every time we eat part of a plant or animal we ingest millions of genes and thus the DNA they are made of. They have no effect on us, however, because they are either broken down as the food is digested or, if they are contained in resistant structures such as seeds, they pass unchanged through the body and are excreted. We have been consuming genes ever since we first evolved and there is no evidence that they can enter human cells from the food we eat. Even if they could,

---

Every time we eat part of a plant or animal we ingest millions of genes and thus the DNA they are made of. They have no effect on us

---

there is nothing to suggest that they would do us any harm.

There is no reason to believe things are any different for any genes in genetically modified (GM) food. Even though certain changes are introduced to the genes, the building blocks of the DNA are exactly the same. It should be clear, however, that in this context, we are talking about several different things. Firstly there are GM products that are eaten more or less unprocessed – for example a tomato in which a gene helping it to ripen has been inactivated to increase its shelf life. These products will contain intact, modified genes when they are consumed. As with non-modified genes, they are broken down as the food is digested.

In processed foods such as tomato purée or soya flour, all genes (including any modified ones) are denatured and inactivated by the processing. Products extracted from plants such as sugars or oils may come from genetically modified plants, but they contain no genes and are identical to the same products extracted from unmodified plants. Finally there are foods whose production involves the use of enzymes derived from GM sources. A familiar example is 'vegetarian' cheese, made with an enzyme (chymosin) from a genetically modified micro-organism, which is the same enzyme as the one of animal origin found in calf rennet. Here the modified genes never come into contact with the food.

Given these several different interpretations of GM food, confusion amongst the public is not surprising, especially when linked to mistaken ideas about what genes are and what they do. It also explains why 72% of those surveyed in the public consultation mentioned above said that they received too little information on these developments and how they are regulated.

Reference
1. *The Public Consultation on Developments in the Biosciences.* Commissioned by the Department of Trade and Industry from MORI.

Have we gone too far in manipulating nature?

Information from the Food Commission

What is genetic engineering?

Genetic engineering involves the dismantling and recombining of genes in the laboratory. A gene is a sequence of bases on a DNA strand that results in the expression of a certain trait. There can be several alleles, or types, of a gene. Genes and gene fragments from one organism can, using appropriate biotechnological methods, be incorporated into the genes of another organism. The donor and recipient organisms do not have to be from the same species, but can be as different as bacteria and mammals, rodents and corn, insects and potatoes. The expression of that inserted gene can be enhanced using promoter gene fragments, often taken from viruses.

Genetically modified foods

Conventional breeding of crops and animals involves artificial selection. In artificial selection, matings are arranged to produce organisms with desirable alleles that therefore express desirable traits. However, conventional breeding is limited in the traits that it can produce. Generally, organisms from different species can't exchange genes because they can't mate with each other. However, genetic engineering allows for the creation of transgenic organisms, or organisms that have genes from other species. Genetically modified foods can have genes from different species or modified genes from within their own species.

Genetically modified foods that are currently on the market in Britain include a tomato paste made from tomatoes that are engineered so that they don't get squishy, maize that is resistant to both insects and to herbicides (weed/plant killers), and soya that is resistant to the herbicide glyphosate .

Labelling – you should have a right to know

For ethical, health, or environmental reasons, some people don't want to eat genetically modified foods. Everyone should have a right to know whether a food product contains genetically modified ingredients. However, the labelling regulations in Europe (and elsewhere) are too weak.

The EC's Council Regulation No. 1139/98 states that all foods containing genetically modified soya or maize must be labelled, except where no modified protein or DNA is present. The regulation does not apply to 'food additives, flavourings for use in foodstuffs or extraction solvents used in the production of foodstuffs'. Soya additives are present in many processed foods.

• The above information is an extract from the Food Commission's web site which can be found at www.foodcomm.org.uk

Food giants accused over GM cover-up

10 per cent of products are tainted without saying so on the label. By Sean Poulter, Consumer Affairs Correspondent

One in ten foods on sale in high street stores contains GM ingredients without declaring details on the label, an investigation has revealed.

Everyday products such as bread, cakes, burgers, ready meals, soya products and crisps were involved, sold at a wide range of outlets and including household names.

The major supermarkets claim to have removed GM ingredients from their own-brand products in response to customer concerns. But the discovery of the deception – which is a criminal offence – makes it clear manufacturers and retailers are failing to carry out proper checks.

EU rules allow foods to contain up to 1 per cent GM ingredients without declaring the fact on the label. Trading standards officers found, however, that a tenth of the foods they examined were above this limit.

More the 5 per cent of the soya present in one product was genetically modified. Friends of the Earth said the survey was 'very worrying'.

'People have made it very clear that they don't want to eat GM food and now the labelling regulations are failing them,' spokesman Carol Kearney added yesterday.

'More rigorous enforcement is needed. If people want to avoid GM food, the safest bet is to buy organic food.'

The monitoring and enforcement of GM contamination and labelling rules is down to trading standards officers, who work for local authorities but often lack the necessary expertise or resources. If prosecuted and convicted, companies could be fined £2,000, although 'naming and shaming' them would have a far bigger impact.

There is no evidence that GM products harm human health, although critics argue that more research is needed.

There are, however, issues of customer information and choice as many consumers want GM-free food on principle.

EU rules allow foods to contain up to 1 per cent GM ingredients without declaring the fact on the label. Trading standards officers found, however, that a tenth of the foods they examined were above this limit

There is also support for Prince Charles's fear that the new technology interferes with nature.

While there is no suggestion that manufacturers are deliberately using GM ingredients, it appears there are problems in the supply chain.

Many companies have systems to separate GM and non-GM ingredients but consignments can be mixed accidentally in bulk container ships, lorries and port storage facilities.

Contamination can even happen while crops are in the ground from GM pollen blown from fields two or three miles away.

The study testing 40 random products was carried out in Kent by Medway Council's public protection team but its results are thought to reflect problems nationwide.

A spokesman said: 'Traces of GM products were found that had not been identified and the results were forwarded to those responsible.'

The council refused to identify the manufacturers and stores involved, but said that it had issued warnings demanding improvements.

© *The Daily Mail*
August, 2001

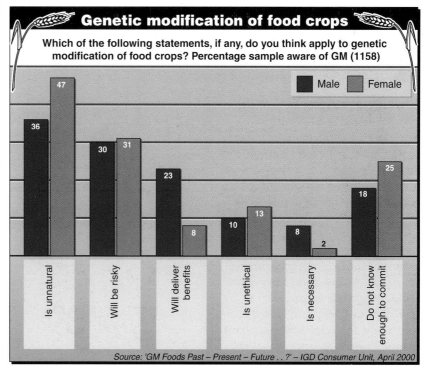

Genetic modification of food crops

Which of the following statements, if any, do you think apply to genetic modification of food crops? Percentage sample aware of GM (1158)

Male | Female

	Is unnatural	Will be risky	Will deliver benefits	Is unethical	Is necessary	Do not know enough to commit
Male	36	30	23	10	8	18
Female	47	31	8	13	2	25

Source: 'GM Foods Past – Present – Future . . ?' – IGD Consumer Unit, April 2000

Consumer concerns over GM labelling

Information from the National Consumer Council

New research released today by the National Consumer Council shows clear consumer support for the 'right to know' whether food is from genetically modified (GM) crops or is the produce of animals fed GM feed. Almost two-thirds (64%) thought it was important that food containing GM ingredients is labelled and over three-quarters (79%) thought that meat and other products from animals fed GM feed should be labelled.

This week, the Council urged the Food Standards Agency (FSA) to support the European Commission's proposals to extend and strengthen GM labelling. In September 2001, the FSA board met to discuss their views on the plans. The proposals cover the approval, labelling and traceability of GM foods and threshold levels for accidental contamination of food by GM crops. They will also extend, for the first time, to animal feed and ingredients made from GM material but in which the modified DNA has been destroyed during processing (known as GM derivatives).

Whilst welcoming the European plans, NCC is concerned that some of the proposals do not go far enough. For instance:

Threshold levels for the amount of accidental contamination by GM crops

The European Commission proposes to maintain a maximum threshold of 1% accidental GM contamination. NCC's survey shows zero contamination is the ideal: 42% of those who had a view expressed this preference. NCC recognises that zero contamination may not be technically possible but believes that, as detection methods and monitoring systems improve, the 1% threshold should be reviewed and preferably lowered.

NCC National **Consumer Council**

Making all consumers matter

Allowing small amounts of accidental contamination by some GM crops, which have not been fully approved for use in the EU

It is worrying that the EU proposes to allow small levels of accidental contamination of food by GM crops and ingredients that are not yet fully approved for use in EU countries. The Council recommends that all GM varieties should receive the same degree of assessment and approval otherwise consumer confidence could be undermined.

The lack of a requirement to label meat and other products from animals fed with GM feed

Although the EU proposals will, for the first time, extend GM labelling to animal feed, there are no immediate plans to label the products of animals fed GM feed. However, NCC's survey showed that almost 8 out of 10 (79%) of people thought that meat and other products from animals fed with GM feed should carry this information. The NCC is therefore urging the FSA to draw up legally-binding industry guidelines for the labelling of products indicating whether or not animals have been fed GM feed.

'This is not consumers wanting "ever more" information; our survey shows consumers have a clear sense of priorities for food labels'

Interestingly, where animals were the issue, consumers' concerns seemed to be heightened. The number of consumers who thought that meat and other products from GM feed should be labelled (79%) is substantially higher than the number of people (64%) who were concerned about labelling food from GM plants. This may be due to the recent crises of BSE and foot-and-mouth disease which have heightened consumers' concerns about what animals are eating.

NCC Chairman, Deirdre Hutton, said: 'Our survey shows that consumers do care about whether or not their food contains GM ingredients and these plans to strengthen and extend GM labelling should help restore consumer confidence. We have spoken to the FSA and hope they will not only support the proposals but go even further so that consumers' concerns are fully addressed. We shall be lobbying European decision makers directly on these important issues.

'This is not consumers wanting "ever more" information; our survey shows consumers have a clear sense of priorities for food labels. Their top three priorities are information on nutritional value, allergic reactions and a full list of ingredients. GM comes next but, even so, a remarkably high number of people (33%) think such labelling is important.'

The Council is also calling for clear liability legislation for GM in the event of damage to the environment, health or trade and more consumer involvement in the risk assessment process.

• The above information is from the National Consumer Council's web site which can be found at www.ncc.org.uk Or see their postal address details on page 41.

© *National Consumer Council 19/09/01*

Watchdog 'is letting food firms cover up GM use'

The official food watchdog has been accused of trying to allow firms to cover up the use of GM ingredients.

The Food Standards Agency (FSA) wants to water down EU proposals that would force the food industry to identify all derivatives from genetically modified crops on packet labels.

Critics say the agency is flying in the face of promises by the Government to adopt a policy of openness and honesty on GM foods.

It has fuelled suspicions that the interests of the biotech industry are being given precedence over those of consumers.

The European Commission is currently consulting the FSA and similar bodies in other member countries on whether to go ahead with the introduction of the regulations on labelling GM derivatives.

The FSA's board voted this week not to accept the proposals. Its decision was condemned by two leading consumer champions, the Consumers' Association and the National Consumer Council.

They warned that derivatives of GM soya and maize, such as lecithin and modified starch, could be used in thousands of foods, from chocolate biscuits to baked beans and bread, without details appearing on labels.

NCC chairman Deirdre Hutton said: 'I am frankly amazed that the FSA has decided not to support the extension of GM labelling to GM derivatives. It flies in the face of what consumers want.'

She said a survey by her organisation found that a clear majority of the British public wanted information on the packets about which GM derivatives were used.

Sue Davies, of the Consumers' Association, said the group was 'appalled' that the FSA was not backing the proposals.

'It seems that at last the

By Sean Poulter, Consumer Affairs Correspondent

European Commission is putting consumer interests first, but sadly, while the FSA is re-stating its commitment to consumer choice and information, its actions in this case appear to indicate a different attitude,' she added.

> **Many consumers believe insufficient work has been done to assess the health and environmental impact of GM crops on humans, wildlife and the countryside**

FSA chairman Sir John Krebs defended the organisation's decision, saying it could prove expensive for food firms to change labels in line with the proposals.

'The agency wants consumers to have real choices on GM and meaningful information,' he said. 'However, there are serious questions of practicality, affordability and enforceability with the proposals.'

Some experts say the FSA appear to have accepted the view of the biotech industry and food firms that GM derivatives are chemically the same as the derivatives from non-modified crops.

They argue, however, that that does not take account of the fact that consumers may wish to exercise their choice not to support GM technology and farming.

Many consumers believe insufficient work has been done to assess the health and environmental impact of GM crops on humans, wildlife and the countryside.

Secrecy surrounding the use of GM ingredients in food products, which arrived on supermarket shelves without any debate, was one of the primary causes of the public backlash against the technology.

*© The Daily Mail
September, 2001*

Genetically engineered crops will help feed the world

By the year 2050 there are likely to be 9 billion people on this Earth, an increase of 50 per cent over the present day. Most of this increase will occur in the cities of developing countries, primarily in Asia. If present economic development continues, this population increase will require a doubling in food production. Only a fraction of the food that all these people will need can be produced in the breadbaskets of the world. Most of this food has to be grown locally. The problem of feeding all the people is worsened by the uneven distribution of cropland. For example, China has a quarter of the human population but only 7 per cent of the world's farmland.

During the last doubling of the human population from 3 billion in 1960 to 6 billion in 2000, food production increases kept up with population growth because we created and adopted multiple new technologies. Better techniques to cultivate the soil, new irrigation technologies, more advanced pesticides that are biodegradable, better genetic strains, machinery that harvests more of the crop, synthetic fertilisers, and green manures that restore the nutrients to the soil all have helped raise food production.

GM crops are only part of the answer

GM crops are not the magic bullet that will feed the world. But they can certainly help because they are an integral part of our continuing quest for the genetic improvement of crops. We can't afford to reject this technology as some are advocating. Progress must be made in other technologies as well. We need more durable, longer-lasting disease and insect resistance, irrigation systems that waste less water, agronomic systems with multiple crops that limit erosion on sloping land. We need to find out which types of soil tilling,

Glossary

Genetic engineering: changing the genetic make-up of an organism using molecular techniques. This includes introducing one or more genes from unrelated organisms.

Genetic modification (GM): often used interchangeably with genetic engineering although there are many types of genetic modification that do not involve genetic engineering.

GM foods: foods derived entirely or in part from GM crops.

fertiliser application, and crop rotation produce the healthiest soils with the most beneficial microbial activity. We need to learn so many things, and yet financial support for agricultural research has been slowly eroding for twenty years.

GM crops cannot eliminate poverty and hunger because these problems are rooted in the socio-political realm. People need jobs to purchase food and with economic demand food production usually picks up. Although the world does indeed produce enough food to eliminate hunger, we have not yet devised an economic system that permits the distribution of that food in an equitable way.

Technologies are not an unmitigated blessing, especially when they are first introduced. Cars pollute the air and people are killed in accidents, but few people want to be without an automobile. Agricultural technologies also have negative effects. To make them better requires our human ingenuity. President Jimmy Carter said so well: 'Responsible biotechnology is not the enemy; starvation is.'

• The above information is from the San Diego Center for Molecular Agriculture (SDCMA) whose web site can be found at www.sdcma.org

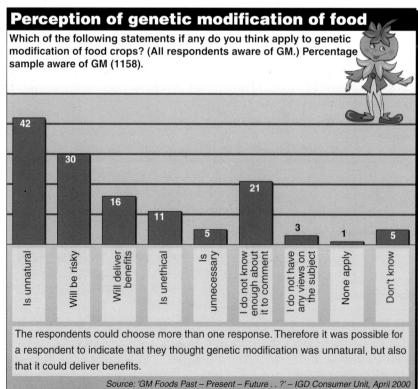

Perception of genetic modification of food

Which of the following statements if any do you think apply to genetic modification of food crops? (All respondents aware of GM.) Percentage sample aware of GM (1158).

Is unnatural	Will be risky	Will deliver benefits	Is unethical	Is unnecessary	I do not know enough about it to comment	I do not have any views on the subject	None apply	Don't know
42	30	16	11	5	21	3	1	5

The respondents could choose more than one response. Therefore it was possible for a respondent to indicate that they thought genetic modification was unnatural, but also that it could deliver benefits.

Source: 'GM Foods Past – Present – Future . . ?' – IGD Consumer Unit, April 2000

GM food products can save lives

Genetic manipulation of food products provokes strong emotions whenever the subject is discussed. So far, this discussion has mainly taken place in Europe and North America, and for too long it has been portrayed as a conflict between commercial interests and consumer interests.

But those who argue for or against genetically modified foods are being left behind by developments on the farm as well as in the laboratories.

GM foods are already here, and research on genetic manipulation of food is taking place in thousands of universities and private companies not only in the industrialised world, but also in a number of other developing nations.

Genetic manipulation

Seen from a farm in Africa and China, the issues look considerably different from the perspective of Western supermarket aisles. Many poor farmers who hear that the GM seeds can increase yields, withstand drought or protect crops from insects, only ask: 'When can we get our hands on these new varieties?'

GM foods have the potential to bring with them the largest change in food production, since the green revolution of the 1960s. We may see vitamin A and iron deficiencies being drastically reduced through GM crops that are rich in such substances.

Iron deficiency might affect four to five billion people worldwide, constituting a public health condition of epidemic proportions. Vitamin A deficiency affects between 100 and 400 million children in the world, leaving 250,000 to 500,000 blind every year, half of them dying within 12 months of losing their sight.

Adding nutrients to food products is not a new idea. Most countries in the world have added iodine to salt for decades to avoid goiter and mental disabilities that are caused by iodine deficiency. Many of the breakfast cereals and other foods on our table have vitamins added to them.

Bio-pharmaceuticals

What is new is that, in this case, scientists are not adding substances – they move genes so the plants produce their own. Down the road, some suggest we may even see 'bio-pharmaceuticals' – food products such as fruits that contain vaccines against diseases. In countries that struggle with low immunisation rates, such products may become major lifesavers.

GM foods have the potential to bring with them the largest change in food production, since the green revolution of the 1960s

---

However, such claims from the investors will not be taken at face value. The efficiency of foods to combat vitamin A deficiency, and produce other positive health effects, needs to be compared to other existing methods to promote health.

We may also encounter serious negative effects. If GM products are more expensive than existing ones, they may not reach the poor. If they are not properly tested, they may have dangerous and unexpected side effects.

Safety concerns

Safety is a key issue, but we may also answer questions about whether genetically modified food is beneficial and for whom.

Since they are more resistant to insects, the new varieties use less insecticides and therefore are more environmentally friendly.

All in all, the scope of any future evaluation should be broad and include safety, nutritional and environmental aspects as well as efficiency, socio-economic and ethical considerations.

Such considerations will be developed with other World Health Organisation (WHO) partners, including such intergovernmental organisations as the United Nations (UN) Food and Agriculture Organisation, UN Environmental Programme, Organisation for Economic Cooperation and Development, the World Bank and non-governmental organisations.

© 2001 World Health Organisation

UN agency backs GM food crops

Grassroots groups angered by conclusion that the poor and the hungry will benefit

By John Vidal and
John Aglionby

The United Nations Development Programme says that many developing countries may reap great benefits from genetically modified foodstuffs, that the technology can significantly reduce the malnutrition which affects 800m people, and that it will be especially valuable to poor farmers working marginal land in sub-Saharan Africa.

The report is one of the agency's most provocative, and grassroots groups, development charities and environmentalists in more than 50 countries described it as 'simplistic', 'pandering to the GM industry' and 'failing to take into account the views of the poor'.

Published yesterday, it says there is an urgent need to develop 'modern' varieties of millet, sorghum and cassava, the staple foods of millions in developing countries. But it says that commercial research mostly caters for the needs of high earners, and it urges greater public investment in GM research and development to ensure that it meets the needs of the poor.

Mark Malloch Brown, the agency's administrator, said recently developed new varieties of rice had 50% higher yields, matured 30-50 days earlier, were substantially richer in protein, and were far more disease and drought resistant.

'They will be especially useful because they can be grown without fertiliser or herbicides, which many poor farmers cannot afford,' he said.

The report said GM risks could be managed, but most developing countries would need help doing so.

Biotechnology and food safety problems were often the result of poor policies and inadequate regulations, it said.

Oxfam, Greenpeace International, Actionaid, the Intermediate Technology Development Group and more than 290 grassroots groups around the world objected strongly to the report's conclusions.

'It diverts attention from other technologies and farming practices that could also raise productivity,' Kevin Watkins, policy director of Oxfam, said.

'It ignores the fact that most hungry people live in countries with food surpluses rather than deficits, and overlooks the fact that companies like Du Pont and Monsanto have sought to discover transgenic manipulations designed solely to enhance the value of their own patents.'

'Complex problems of hunger and agricultural development will not be solved by technological silver bullets,' Von Hernandez of Greenpeace South-east Asia said.

'The real crisis is the neglect of research and investment in the development of sustainable and ecological agriculture technologies. The UNDP has reduced its support for traditional agriculture and is now insisting on GM crops as a means of "helping humanity".'

Robert Vint of Genetic Food Alert, speaking on behalf of 290 groups in 54 developing countries which disagree with the report and do not want to see GM crops in their countries, said: 'It contains frightening echoes of recent biotechnology industry propaganda.'

Klaus Leisinger of the Novartis Foundation, which was set up by the GM company Novartis, described Greenpeace as 'Luddites' and urged reliance on 'good science'.

'Let's support public research and not prevent field trials,' he said. 'The myths have trickled down. This is an ideology with people on both sides trying to prove their case.'

The main author of the report, Sakiko Fukuda-Parr, defended her work. 'I think the first-world environmentalists should put on the shoes of a farmer in Mali faced with crop

failures every other year and think what technological development could do for his harvest,' she said.

Meanwhile in Bangkok the deputy prime minister, John Prescott, told an international biotech meeting organised by the British government and the Organisation for Economic Cooperation and Development that the world would eventually support GM crop production because it was 'widely agreed that it has tremendous benefits'.

The meeting was boycotted by many grassroots groups, and Mr Prescott's views were not shared by the Thai deputy prime minister, Suwit Khunkitti, who said Thailand would not embrace agricultural biotechnology until it was scientifically proved that it could benefit all people.

'I insist that Thailand stays neutral,' he said. 'Scientists must prove that genetically altered foods

increase yields and are safe to humans and the environment in the long run.'

Two hundred members of five organisations, grouped under the

Thai People's Network against GMO, demonstrated outside the venue and distributed GM food.

Seeds of conflict

GM crops are being grown in 13 countries and tested or developed in dozens more

For:
- They could significantly increase yields and raise incomes, lifting people out of poverty and providing food security
- Health benefits, such as extra vitamins, can be engineered in
- They could help farmers cultivate marginal land prone to drought or salt
- They could help the environment by reducing the need for herbicides and pesticides
- They benefit corporations and Western shareholders

Against:
- May be unsuitable for poor farmers who could become locked into a technology they cannot control
- Expensive: could force farmers into debt and prevent them saving seed
- Land reform, manure and traditional breeding techniques could deliver more benefits
- Many claims are exaggerated or unproved. Reduced use of chemicals is debatable

---

Advisers warn GM crop tests 'not final piece in jigsaw'

By John Vidal

The government's farm-scale trials of GM crops will not provide enough evidence to allow them to be grown commercially, says a key advisory body.

The agriculture and environment biotechnology commission, set up by the government last year and made up of industrialists, ecologists and academics, believed the 240-odd trials now taking place around Britain were hurriedly designed in a secretive way, with key players not fully engaged.

The 20-strong commission, which admits great differences of opinion among its members, agreed that the trials should continue but said that they posed a threat to the legal status of organic farmers and might be fuelling growing disrespect for government policy while raising further ecological concerns.

In its first detailed report, the commission recommended that there should be wider separation distances between GM crops and conventional

ones and far more public consultation.

'They cannot be the final piece of the jigsaw before commercialisation can proceed. Additional information and considerations must be factors in the eventual decision.'

It also recommended an independent survey of all scientific, ecological and social evidence be carried out before approvals are given, possibly next year.

The trials have been controversial from the start and many have been partially or wholly damaged by protestors. 'The government is fully aware that the information which will be provided from the trials will be limited, yet statements by ministers have not always made this clear,' the report said.

'The crops have become a lightning rod for people's concerns about GM technology,' it added.

The report urges the government to take into account matters such as scientific information from other sources, ethical concerns, and the economic issues, which will be raised by the forthcoming review of British agriculture.

'The GM trials have always been far more about politics than rigorous science,' said Pete Riley of Friends of the Earth yesterday.

He added: 'The government should abandon the trials and recognise that they cannot impose GM crops and food on a public which does not want them.'

'This report shows the trial sites process has been ill-conceived and flawed from the start,' said Patrick Holden, director of the Soil Association. 'It recognises that the trials threaten the organic status of farmers across the country. The government must act on its findings as a matter of urgency.'

GM meat 'will be on the market within 10 years'

By James Chapman, Science Correspondent

Meat from the first genetically-modified farm animals will be on our plates within ten years, leading scientists are predicting.

Experts at the Royal Society believe that livestock engineered to be resistant to foot-and-mouth and other diseases could offer major benefits.

GM pork from pigs that have been given cow genes will be the first to make it to the supermarket shelves in the UK, according to Professor Ian McConnell.

Such pigs have been genetically modified to have 'an antimicrobial protein' in their milk, said the veterinary scientist from Cambridge University.

'Piglets that suckle on them have a much reduced incidence of gastro-intestinal disease, which is a terrible problem,' he explained, adding: 'These pigs exist, and will have to go through the proper licensing authorities.

'Everything will be tested to see if these animals are safe to eat before they get onto the market place.' Prof McConnell, speaking ahead of the publication today of a report from the Royal Society on the issue of GM animals, said that the sale of modified pork was about 'ten years away'.

The report's authors predict that GM animals will become as controversial as GM crops and admit there are risks.

They include new or increased allergic reactions in humans who eat GM meat. Other animals could suffer from effects on GM animals, including increased aggression.

Creatures engineered to carry human strains of disease might act as reservoirs of infection should they escape into the environment.

The experts are particularly worried about the development of GM salmon which grow up to ten times faster than normal. They could escape into the wild and devastate native shoals.

Despite the concerns, the report concludes that the potential benefits outweigh the risks.

Animals engineered to be 'models' for human disease had been a crucial part of medical research for more than 20 years, it says.

GM pork from pigs that have been given cow genes will be the first to make it to the supermarket shelves in the UK

Professor Patrick Bateson, vice-president of the Royal Society and chairman of the working group behind the report, said: 'We now know that animals such as the mouse share many of the 30,000 to 40,000 human genes.

'Animals that can be genetically modified to develop human diseases, such as cancer, muscular dystrophy and cystic fibrosis, are increasingly important in assessing new therapies which one day may relieve the suffering of millions of patients.

'We are already seeing the benefits of this research through the production of such substances as human blood-clotting factors.'

On genetically tinkering with the make-up of animals for food, Prof Bateson argued that it was simply a more precise version of selective breeding.

He launched an attack on Prince Charles, who has warned of the 'potentially disastrous consequences' of genetic technology.

'There will certainly be people who say we are playing God,' said Prof Bateson. 'Our response would be that we have been playing God for an awfully long time.

'The idyllic organic farms that Prince Charles would like us to have all have animals that have been genetically modified for thousands of years. The horse he rides has been genetically modified, the hounds that ride by their sides have been genetically modified. It is not a new issue.'

He added that the move towards GM animals would be partially consumer-driven.

'There will be companies that try to develop things like salmonella-free chicken,' he said. 'And everybody wants cattle that are resistant against foot-and-mouth.'

Though the idea of moving genes between species seemed 'ghastly', Prof Bateson insisted: 'Genomes are not that different from each other. We share 30 per cent of our genes with a banana.'

Acknowledging concerns about the GM issue, the report recommends the Government funds more studies.

Laboratories carrying out GM research should have emergency plans in the event of animals escaping. The RS, Britain's academy of science, also wants a moratorium on GM fish research except in cages in land-locked lakes.

© *The Daily Mail*
May, 2001

ADDITIONAL RESOURCES

You might like to contact the following organisations for further information. Due to the increasing cost of postage, many organisations cannot respond to enquiries unless they receive a stamped, addressed envelope.

Animal Aid
The Old Chapel
Bradford Street
Tonbridge, TN9 1AW
Tel: 01732 364546
Fax: 01732 366533
E-mail: info@animalaid.org.uk
Web site: www.animalaid.org.uk
Animal Aid is the UK's largest animal rights group. They campaign against all forms of animal abuse and promote a cruelty-free lifestyle.

CropGen
31 St Petersburg Place
London, W2 4LA
Tel: 0845 602 1793
Fax: 020 7853 2306
E-mail: info@cropgen.org
Web site: www.cropgen.org
CropGen's mission is to make the case for GM crops by helping to achieve a greater measure of realism and better balance in the UK public debate about crop biotechnology.

European Food Information Council (EUFIC)
1 Place des Pyramides 75001
Paris, France
Tel: 00 33 140 20 44 40
Fax: 00 33 140 20 44 41
E-mail: eufic@eufic.org
Web site: www.eufic.org
EUFIC has been established to provide science-based information on foods and food-related topics i.e. nutrition and health, food safety and quality and biotechnology in food for the attention of European consumers.

The Food Commission
94 White Lion Street
London, N1 9PF
Tel: 020 7837 2250
Fax: 020 7837 1141
E-mail: enquiries@foodcomm.org.uk
Web site: www.foodcomm.org.uk
Committed to ensuring good quality food for all. They are a national non-profit organisation campaigning for the right to safe, wholesome food.

Friends of the Earth (FOE)
26-28 Underwood Street
London, N1 7JQ
Tel: 020 7490 1555
Fax: 020 7490 0881
E-mail: info@foe.co.uk
Web site: www.foe.co.uk
As an independent environmental group, Friends of the Earth publishes a comprehensive range of leaflets, books and in-depth briefings and reports.

Greenpeace
Canonbury Villas
London, N1 2PN
Tel: 020 7865 8100
Fax: 020 7865 8200
E-mail: gn-info@uk.greenpeace.org
Web site: www.greenpeace.org.uk
Greenpeace is an independent non-profit global campaigning organisation that uses non-violent, creative confrontation to expose global environmental problems and causes.

John Innes Centre
Norwich Research Park
Colney, Norwich, NR4 7UH
Tel: 01603 450000
Fax: 01603 450045
Web site: www.jic.bbsrc.ac.uk
Europe's premier independent centre for research and training in plant and microbial science.

Monsanto UK Limited
Suite 23, Tulip House
70 Borough High Street
London, SE1 1XF
Tel: 020 7864 9913
Fax: 020 7495 8361
Web site: www.monsanto.co.uk
Monsanto is committed to finding solutions to the growing global needs for food and health by sharing common forms of science and technology among agriculture, nutrition and health.

National Consumers Council
20 Grosvenor Gardens
London, SW1W 0DH
Tel: 020 7730 3469
Fax: 020 7730 0191
E-mail: info@ncc.org.uk

Web site: www.ncc.org.uk
A research and policy organisation providing a vigorous and independent voice for domestic consumers in the UK.

National Farmers' Union (NFU)
164 Shaftesbury Avenue
London, WC2H 8HL
Tel: 020 7331 7200
Fax: 020 7331 7313
E-mail: nfu@nfu.org.uk
Web site: www.nfu.org.uk
The NFU is the democratic organisation representing farmers and growers in England and Wales.

Society, Religion and Technology Project
Church of Scotland, John Knox House, 45 High Street
Edinburgh, EH1 1SR
Tel: 0131 556 2953
Fax: 0131 556 7478
E-mail: srtp@srtp.org.uk
Web site: www.srtp.org.uk
Works to foster an informed understanding in society of the issues of current and future technologies.

The Soil Association
Bristol House, 40-56 Victoria Street
Bristol, BS1 6BY
Tel: 0117 929 0661
Fax: 0117 925 2504
E-mail: info@soilassociation.org
Web site: www.soilassociation.org
Works to educate the general public about organic agriculture, gardening and food, and their benefits for both human health and the environment.

Young People's Trust for the Environment (YPTENC)
8 Leapale Road
Guildford, GU1 4JX
Tel: 01483 539600
Fax: 01483 301992
E-mail: info@yptenc.org.uk
Web site: www.yptenc.org.uk
The Young People's Trust for the Environment is a charity which aims to encourage young people's understanding of the environment and of the need for sustainability.

INDEX

ACKNOWLEDGEMENTS

The publisher is grateful for permission to reproduce the following material.

While every care has been taken to trace and acknowledge copyright, the publisher tenders its apology for any accidental infringement or where copyright has proved untraceable. The publisher would be pleased to come to a suitable arrangement in any such case with the rightful owner.

Chapter One: An Overview

Genetically modified foods, © Young People's Trust for the Environment (YTENC), *Pros and cons*, © Church of Scotland Society, Religion and Technology Project, *GM crops concern*, © IGD Consumer Unit, *The concerns*, © The Food Commission, *The benefits*, © The Food Commission.

Chapter Two: The GMF Debate

The debate nobody wants, © Guardian Newspapers Limited 2001, *Public Concern*, © Mintel International, *The great food gamble*, © Friends of the Earth (FOE), *GM foods may be present in your food without your knowledge*, © Soil Association, *Genetically modified organisms (GMOs)*, © National Farmers' Union (NFU), *GM tomato could reduce cancer risk*, © Telegraph Group Limited, London 2001, *The risks*, © The Food Commission, *Biotechnology benefits*, © 2001 Monsanto Company, *Growing 20 times faster, the GM oranges*, © The Daily Mail, March 2001, *Genetically modified food – key issues*, © Soil Association, *The case for crop biotechnology*, © CropGen, *GM crops*, © Crown copyright is reproduced with the permission of the Controller of Her Majesty's Stationery Office, *Is GE food safe?*, © Anup Shah, *GM decision condemned by consumer groups*, © National Consumer Council (NCC), *GM foods affect your life*, © Reproduced with permission from The University of California San Diego, *Food production: old and new*, © John Innes Centre, *Questions and answers*, © Animal Aid, *What do you think, if any, are the possible risks or drawbacks of genetic modification of crops?*, © IGD Consumer Unit, *Why do we need them?*, © Green Direct, *Supermarkets*, © Greenpeace, *Biotech primer*, © 2001 Monsanto Company, *Genetic modification of major crops*, © The Food Commission, *Genes in the spotlight*, © European Food Information Council (EUFIC), *Have we gone too far in manipulating nature?*, © The Food Commission, *Food giants accused over GM cover-up*, © The Daily Mail, August 2001, *Genetic modification of food crops*, © IGD Consumer Unit, *Consumer concerns over GM labelling*, © National Consumer Council (NCC), *Watchdog 'is letting food firms cover up GM use'*, © The Daily Mail, September 2001, *Genetically engineered crops will help feed the world*, © Reproduced with permission from The University of California San Diego, *Perception of genetic modification of food*, © IGD Consumer Unit, *GM food products can save lives*, © 2001 World Health Organisation (WHO), *UN agency backs GM food crops*, © Guardian Newspapers Limited 2001, *Advisers warn GM crop tests 'not final piece in jigsaw'*, © Guardian Newspapers Limited 2001, *GM meat 'will be on the market within 10 years'*, © The Daily Mail, May 2001.

Photographs and illustrations:

Pages 1, 11, 13, 24, 35, 38: Pumpkin House, pages 4, 7, 15, 16, 18, 23, 27, 32, 37: Simon Kneebone.

Craig Donnellan
Cambridge
January, 2002